DESIGN DRAWING

WILLIAM KIRBY LOCKARD

EXPERIENCES

FOURTH EDITION, REVISED

PP

PEPPER PUBLISHING

A Division of Arran Enterprises, Ltd.

Library of Congress Cataloging in Publication Data

Lockard, William Kirby, 1929-
 Design drawing experiences/William Kirby Lockard.
4th ed., rev.—Tucson, Ariz.: Pepper Pub., c 1979

 143 p.:chiefly ill. (som col.); 22 x 29 cm

 ISBN 0-914468-07-3

 1. Architectural drawing. 2. Architectural rendering.
3. Drawing. I. Title

 NA2705.L622 1979   720′.28′4   79-65404
                                          MARC

Printed in the United States of America

Published by PEPPER PUBLISHING
            2901 East Mabel Street
            Tucson, Arizona 85716

Library of Congress Catalog card number 79-65404
ISBN: 0-914468-07-3

Available in Spanish from
Editorial Trillas, S.A.
Av. Rio Churubusco 385 Pte.
Apartado Postal 10534
Mexico 13, D.F.

NOTES ON THE REVISED EDITION

In the six years since the original publication of this book I have received a great deal of helpful criticism from students and fellow teachers, and have experienced using the book in my own classes. The present revisions are all based on that criticism, for which I am very grateful, and that experience, which is always instructive.

The book contains more, and hopefully clearer, instructions as well as a greater variety of "experiences." I have replaced what I have judged to be the clever but superficial kind of exercise in favor of the more challenging and fundamental variety, and rearranged the entire book to match the forthcoming revision of the companion text *Design Drawing*. The revised edition also contains several exercises printed on tracing paper to illustrate the overlay technique and to allow blueprinting of the finished drawings.

The most drastic, and I believe, beneficial revisions occur in the central chapters on PERSPECTIVE and LIGHT. In explaining perspective I have returned to the explanation I used earlier in *Drawing as a Means to Architecture* because I believe it is clearer, and almost all the perspective exercises in this edition ask the student to apply the entire method in drawing the perspective of a given space.

The shadow-casting method has been totally revised, and for the first time is completely integrated with the eyelevel perspective method because I believe that it strengthens an understanding of perspective, and because I have found that students have great difficulty in bringing the previous shadow-casting method, which was explained in aerial perspective, down to eyelevel. Shadow casting is also explained as a matter of free choice, which it should always be, rather than the inevitable result of a fixed sun position.

I also believe that printing the explanations of both the perspective and shadow-casting methods in four colors is worthwhile since an understanding of either method depends on clearly perceiving the three sets of perpendicular planes and their vanishing lines.

Once again I would like to thank those of you who took the time to criticize the original edition and invite your critical evaluations of this edition. I also wish to thank my son Scott for helping revise the drawings.

WILLIAM KIRBY LOCKARD
Tucson   1979

TABLE OF CONTENTS

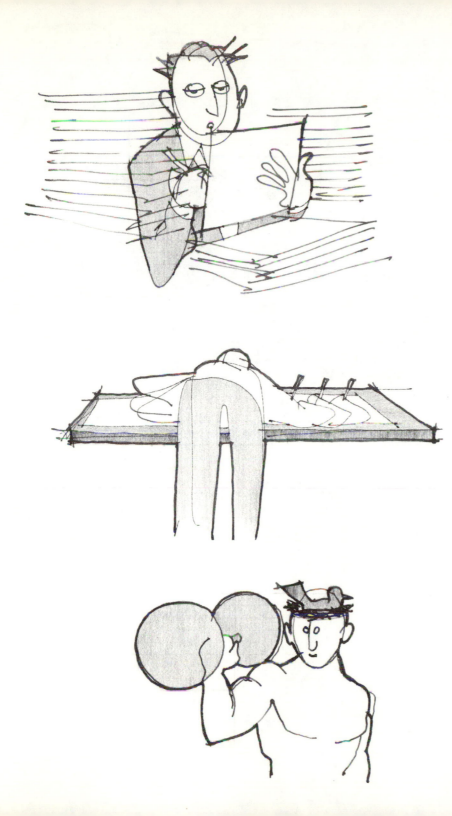

INTRODUCTION

EXERCISES. My experience in teaching drawing is that the development and grading of drawing exercises is a very time-consuming, potentially boring task. Yet, the quality and interest of the exercises, and their careful correction, is basic to any teaching or learning of drawing.

The goal of any set of tasks by which students are to learn to draw, must be to interest, challenge or tease them into making a succession of drawings which they recognize as being successful and worth the effort in the self rewards they bring. Drawing exercises should also leave room for students' personal creativity. Design drawing exercises should ask for and value the students' design contribution, not just ask them to be Xerox machines. The purpose in teaching drawing should be, entirely, to turn a student on to drawing. I hope the drawing tasks in this book will help do that.

While the drawing tasks should be interesting and value design creativity, they should not be permissive. The basic drawing skills to be learned in design drawing are perhaps comparable to the learning of English grammar and spelling. The skills allow you to be eloquent, but first the fundamentals must be mastered; and the teacher must insist that there is a discipline to drawing a line, or casting a shadow or structuring a perspective that is mandatory.

EXPERIENCES. Although drawing is certainly partly physical, I object to the use of the word EXERCISE to describe the assigned tasks which are intended to help a student learn to draw.

EXERCISE carries a suggestion of calisthenics which excludes any thinking or cognitive learning and promotes the Cartesian legacy of mind-body separation. The learning of drawing must rely heavily on actual drawing. No amount of reading or listening to lectures about drawing will teach a student to draw. The assigned drawing tasks, however, would be better renamed EXPERIENCES. I realize that "experiences" is becoming an overused word nowadays, but it does communicate an involvement of body AND mind, and even the emotions, in the simple pleasure of using the body and mind to make a beautiful drawing.

The set of design drawing experiences collected in this book are intended to allow a student to experience the drawing skills presented in the companion book *Design Drawing*. The experiences in this book are intended to be assigned in class and handed in, but must be supported by the theory and instruction in *Design Drawing* or by thorough classroom instruction, based on that book. The companion book, *Design Drawing,* then can be resold or used as a library reference supported by clear classroom instruction.

The experiences are intended to be interesting and rewarding, to allow a student to experience the pleasure of making a drawing he or she recognizes as successful and to help him or her understand exactly how the success was accomplished. Drawing experiences should teach success and confidence — never test to failure.

VARIOUS DESIGNERS. I hope the design drawing experiences which follow will be interesting and appropriate for students of Architecture, Landscape Architecture, and Interior Design. For general design courses and for high school courses, I hope the variety of experiences may allow the student to consider which of these various design disciplines hold the most interest for her or him as a designer.

KINDS OF EXPERIENCES. The various kinds of experiences are categorized and ordered to correspond generally to the text, *Design Drawing*. While there is nothing particularly precious about the order in which they are undertaken, I would recommend that TECHNIQUES and PERSPECTIVE (including shadow-casting) are absolutely basic, should be undertaken early, and completely mastered. The experiences should also be cumulative; that is, once shadow-casting or any other skill has been learned, it should be required on all subsequent drawing assignments.

USE OF THE EXPERIENCES. At the beginning of each set of experiences, there is a brief explanation of the purpose of the particular set, some suggested criteria for evaluation, and one or more examples of the kind of drawing to be produced. In many cases, the instructor may choose to change the assignment or the criteria according to his or her own way of drawing. That is, in fact, valuable because the student will soon realize that there are many ways to draw, and the responsibility of a drawing teacher, or any teacher, is to teach the way he or she thinks is true or best, demanding that the students try that way, but ultimately encouraging them to MAKE their own way of drawing.

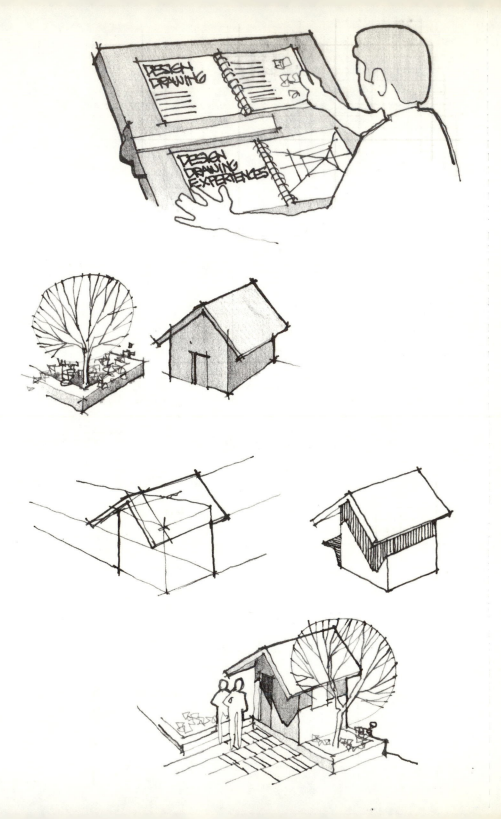

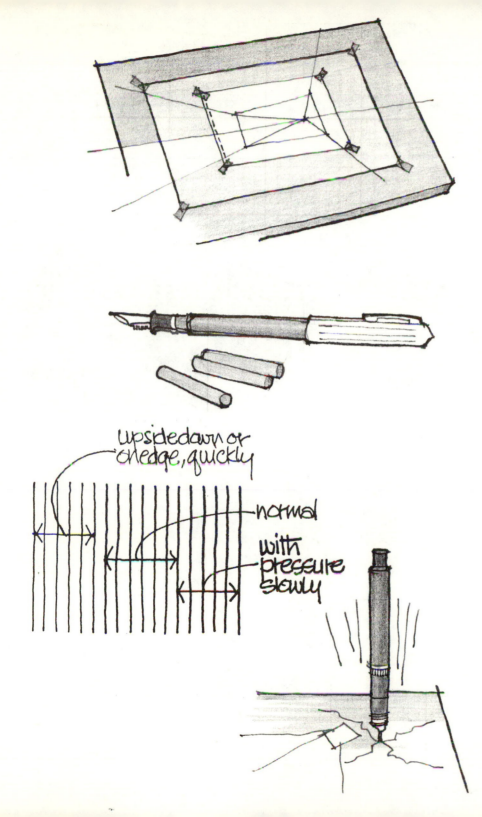

upside down or
on edge, quickly

normal

with
pressure
slowly

Students may work directly on the sheets provided, or the sheets may be overlaid with an 8½″ × 11″ sheet of tracing paper and varied according to additional instructions. Some of the exercises are printed on tracing paper so that after they are completed they may be blueprinted and then colored in order to gain experience in the use of reproduction techniques. Most of the experiences may be supplemented by asking for the delineation of furniture, materials, people, plants, or changing the light assumption. Many of the frameworks are multipurpose and may be used for various combinations of drawing experiences, and many of the frameworks may be expanded spatially to make 10″ × 16″ or larger renderings. The duplicate frameworks on colored paper are intended to allow assignments using "black and white on middle tone" drawing techniques. Another excellent method of teaching drawing is to ask the students to design an experience which promotes learning of a particular drawing skill.

PEN. Books on drawing often spend too much time talking about drawing instruments and paper. Design drawings can be made with your finger in the sand or with literally any marking tool on any surface. To become "implement minded" about drawing is to make the same mistake that the weekend golfer makes in depending on his new set of irons to break 100.

However, for the sake of efficiency and economy I will tell you that many of the drawings in this book were made with an inexpensive Sheaffer cartridge fountain pen. These pens usually are packaged with blue ink cartridges, but you will want JET BLACK ink. Some of my students buy the ink by the bottle and refill their cartridges with a hypodermic syringe.

This simple pen does most of what any expensive pen set will do—and it NEVER clogs. The criteria for any pen is that it make lines of varying widths and by turning the Sheaffer pen over or bearing down hard enough to spread the nibs, it will make all the line widths shown on the right. I have probably owned thirty Sheaffer pens—because I lost them, but I have never destroyed one by driving it into my drawing board in frustration after a half hour's shaking—trying to get it unclogged, as I have several of the more expensive pens. I carry a Sheaffer pen with me habitually and use it to take notes, sign checks, and all the other normal writing tasks. It is very important to design and draw with the same instrument you use for everyday writing. This habit will let you design and draw anywhere, anytime and greatly improve both abilities.

PAPER. The drawings in this book were first sketched and refined on cheap buff tracing paper, then overlaid with fadeout grid tracing paper from an 8½″ × 11″ pad and traced for the final drawing. For completing the assigned experiences, I would recommend you follow the same procedure—using buff tracing paper until you know what you want to draw and then doing the final drawing either on the sheet provided or on an 8½″× 11″ piece of tracing paper. The fadeout grid is handy for writing and for helping you measure and draw horizontal or vertical lines. Most white tracing papers have a coating or finish, however, which does not readily take ink and you will need to buy a can of POUNCE to rub on the paper to give it enough roughness to take the ink.

VARIATIONS. Any of the experiences may be combined with assigned tasks appropriate to the design discipline involved. Interior designers would concentrate on furniture, color and textures. Landscape architects would concentrate on plant materials and landscape elements. Architects would concentrate on architectural materials and structure.

DESIGN CONTENT. Although it is difficult and even harmful to separate DRAWING from DESIGN, our compulsion to sort and categorize produces separate drawing courses in most design curricula. I believe it is mandatory to keep some design content in design drawing courses.

Students should never be asked to turn off their creativity and mindlessly copy a drawing. I hope that the design drawing experiences in this book will always be assigned with instructions to change the object or place represented by the drawing in a direction suggested by the instructor or by the student's own creative intuition.

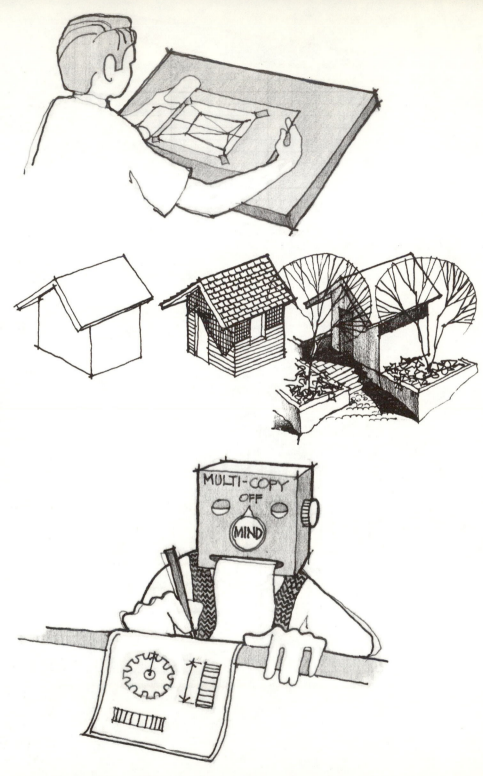

CONCEPTUAL DRAWING

This section of the book will be concerned with drawing's relationship to the design process, particularly the initial conceptual stages of that process. Conceptual drawing is an interactive process which involves all the tools of human intelligence: eye, mind and hand. It is not the neutral "printing out" of a previous, separate conceptual process. Patterns and relationships appear in the drawings unexplained, and if we learn to anticipate, evaluate and use these welcome occurences, we open a new - or rather a very old- dimension of human ability.

Drawing is just as legitimate and useful as a tool for thinking as language or mathematics - it just happens to be neglected in conventional education. While we spend decades teaching our young people to use language and mathematics as tools of thought, we spend little or no time teaching them to think with drawings....even in professional design schools.

You should develop the habit of combining drawing with thinking, and drawing with words so that you are fluent in both and skillful at translating from one to the other. Your conceptual drawings should even develop a personal style and vigor- a pleasure to draw and to look at.

11

ANALOGICAL DRAWING

This set of experiences is designed to help students develop the ability of using analogies and making them graphic. One of the most valuable creative habits is the making of relationships between apparently unrelated ideas.... to see how one thing is like another, especially when they are apparent opposites. The ability to see how a problem, a context or a functional pattern is like something else we know about allows us to make bridges to our knowledge and past experience and use them in solving problems.

Good analogies are often unexpectedly related in depth - beyond their initially obvious like qualities - in secondary levels of detail. Drawing the analogy is one of the best ways to provoke this deeper understanding of a good analogy.

Analogies, when strong ones can be found, are also one of the most effective ways of communicating design ideas to clients.

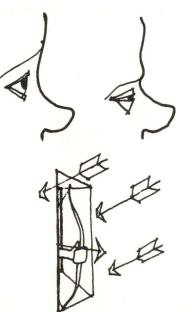

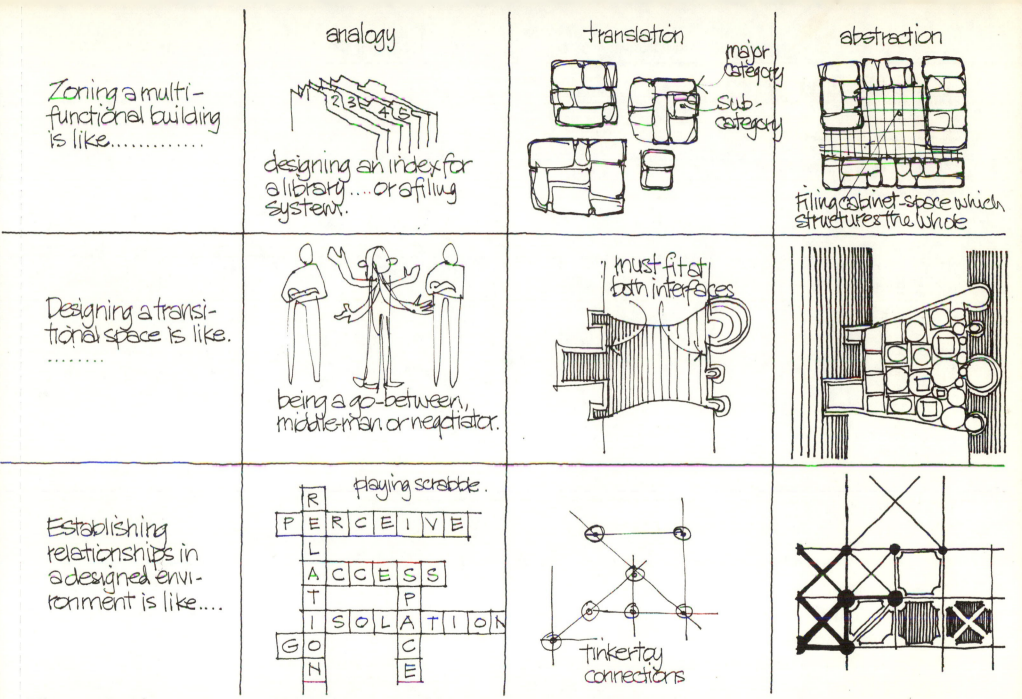

	analogy	translation	abstraction
Zoning a multi-functional building is like...........	designing an index for a library.....or a filing system.	major category / sub-category	Filing cabinet-space which structures the whole
Designing a transitional space is like.	being a go-between, middle-man or negotiator.	must fit at both interfaces	
Establishing relationships in a designed environment is like....	Playing scrabble.	tinkertoy connections	

The analogies above and their translation into abstract diagrams are examples of the analogical drawings asked for in the following exercises. Most analogies must be translated into abstract diagrams before they are useful in the design process.

	analogy	translation	abstraction
PROBLEM Designing an environment which will change in the future is like....			
Designing a flexible, multipurpose space is like..........			
Designing an energy-efficient building is like.............			

Conceive and draw analogies for the problems described at left above. Translate the analogies into graphic abstractions which capture the essence of the analogy and refine these to their strongest forms.

	analogy	translation	abstraction
Designing a proto-typical building which is adaptable to various sites and climates is like........			
Designing an environment on a very tight time schedule is like..............			
Designing an environment which has the goal of maximizing human choice is like..............			

Conceive and draw analogies for the problems described at left above. Translate the analogies into graphic abstractions which capture the essence of the analogy and refine these to their strongest forms.

FUNCTION	analogy	translation	abstraction
A functional pattern which must happen in a particular linear order is like..........			
A functional require-ment that an environ-ment be easily main-tained is like..........			
A functional pattern involving the meeting and private conversa-tion of small groups or individuals is like..			

Conceive and draw analogies for the functions described at left above. Translate the analogies into graphic abstractions which capture the essence of the analogy and refine these to their strongest forms.

	analogy	translation	abstraction
Providing a variety of light, view and privacy options in the design of a window is like.......			
A functional pattern which requires controlled circulation is like................			
The interface between two transportation systems is like...............			

Conceive and draw analogies for the functions described at left above. Translate the analogies into graphic abstractions which capture the essence of the analogy and refine these to their strongest forms.

CONTEXT	analogy	translation	abstraction
A very remote inaccessable natural site is like...............			
Responding to a historic site surrounded by older buildings of great value is like................			
Preserving the exterior of a building while gutting and redesigning the interior is like......			

Conceive and draw analogies for the contexts described at left above. Translate the analogies into graphic abstractions which capture the essence of the analogy and refine these to their strongest forms.

18

	analogy	translation	abstraction
A site with a very undesirable view or orientation along one side is like......			
A very prominent site which can be seen from a great distance is like....			
An oceanfront site is like........			

Conceive and draw analogies for the contexts described at left above. Translate the analogies into graphic abstractions which capture the essence of the analogy and refine these to their strongest forms.

DIRECT DRAWING

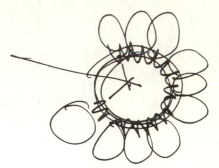

This set of experiences is designed to help students learn to recognize potential patterns and relationships, manipulate them to their best form and communicate them graphically. Unlike analogical drawing this drawing is a direct attempt at graphic expression and the analogy - the similarity to other problems or solutions - is only implied. The patterns and relationships may be a diagram of the problem to be solved, its context, functional pattern or proposed form in plan or section.

Most formal patterns are not self-apparent - at least the more sophisticated ones, and usually not to beginning designers. Like the habit of making analogies, we recognize potential patterns in our designs because we see how they are like, or can be made to be like, other patterns we know about.

This is why good designers usually have an extensive knowledge of historical and contemporary examples of good design in their respective fields - and are quick to recognize the potential patterns and relationships in design problems.

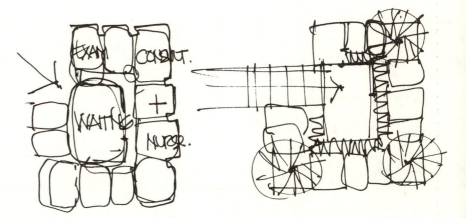

The ability to diagram a context, for instance, depends on some knowledge of what goes to make up any context - sun, wind, vegetation, surrounding buildings, views and pedestrian and automobile traffic - and how these constituents may be related and expressed graphically. The value in drawing the various aspects of a design problem in diagrammatic form is that our minds can see, comprehend and respond to more visual information than we can ever remember from verbal notes.

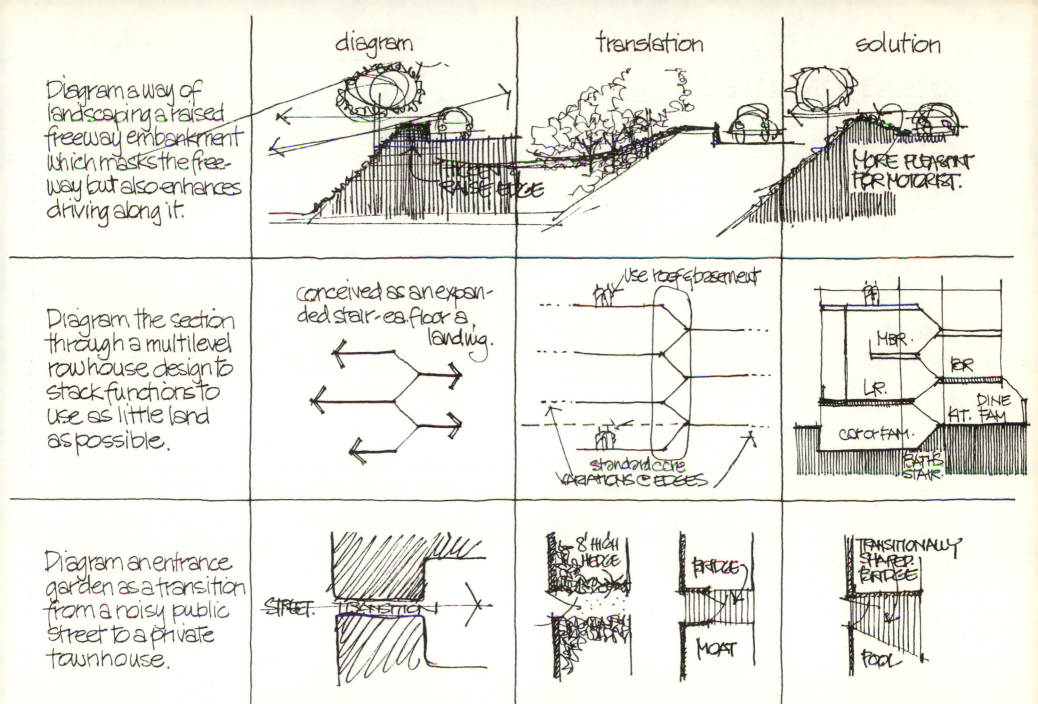

	diagram	translation	solution

Diagram a way of landscaping a raised freeway embankment which masks the free-way but also enhances driving along it.

HIDDEN RAISED EDGE

MORE PLEASANT FOR MOTORIST.

Diagram the section through a multilevel row house design to stack functions to use as little land as possible.

conceived as an expanded stair-ea. floor a landing.

Use roof & basement

standard core VARIATIONS @ EDGES

MBR.
LR.
car or FAM.
BR
KT. FAM
DINE
BATH
STAIR.

Diagram an entrance garden as a transition from a noisy public street to a private townhouse.

STREET. TRANSITION

8 HIGH HEDGE

BRIDGE
MOAT

TRANSITIONALLY SHAPED. BRIDGE
POOL

The diagrams above and their translation into designed environments are examples of the kind of direct drawing asked for in the succeeding exercises. The successful translation of diagrammatic concepts into built form depends on a broad and confident vocabulary of formal and material alternatives.

	diagram	translation	solution
RELATIONSHIPS			
Diagram a complementary relationship between a building and its site.			
Diagram a hierarchical relationship for a group of buildings like a campus.			
Diagram an equivocal or ambiguous relationship between two interior spaces.			

Conceive and draw diagrams which directly express the relationships described at left above. Translate and refine the initial abstract diagrams into designed environments in such a way that the essence and clarity of the original diagram is retained in the designed environment.

	diagram	translation	solution
Diagram the relationship between two dissimilar spaces when it is made by a third transitional space.			
Diagram the relationship of selective control between two spaces.			
Diagram a series of spaces which combine to make a sequence while maintaining their individuality.			

Conceive and draw diagrams which directly express the relationships described at left above. Translate and refine the initial abstract diagrams into designed environments in such a way that the essence and clarity of the original diagram is retained in the designed environment.

	diagram	translation	solution
FUNCTION			
Diagram a cluster of diverse functions which share a common entry point.			
Diagram the problem of adding onto a building whose interior functions need to expand in several places.			
Diagram an exterior space that serves as the transition between 2 quite different buildings.			

Conceive and draw diagrams which directly express the functions described at left above. Translate and refine the initial abstract diagrams into designed environments in such a way that the essence and clarity of the original diagram is retained in the designed environment.

	diagram	translation	solution
Diagram a functional pattern which must separate various kinds of people (doctors, nurses, patients and then bring them together in a controlled way.			
Diagram a pattern through a museum which could be taken in one continuous sequence but allows shortcuts for selective museum-goers.			
Diagram a particular ritual with which you are familiar - a church service, a graduation ceremony etc.			

Conceive and draw diagrams which directly express the functions described at left above. Translate and refine the initial abstract diagrams into designed environments in such a way that the essence and clarity of the original diagram is retained in the designed environment.

CONTEXT	diagram	translation	solution
Diagram a religious sanctuary-closed off from the outside world. Locate altar etc.			
Diagram in section a multi-story building which relates to a busy pedestrian context at ground level then transitions to a distant view response above.			
Diagram a house form which stands in contrast to nature as a man-made object.			

Conceive and draw diagrams which directly express the contexts described at left above. Translate and refine the initial abstract diagrams into designed environments in such a way that the essence and clarity of the original diagram is retained in the designed environment.

	diagram	translation	solution
Diagram a house form which appears to grow out of a heavily wooded, steep hillside in sympathy w/ nature.			
Design earth forms and planting to emphasize a winding walk through a park.			
Diagram a context that changes dramatically in its use from night to day.			

Conceive and draw diagrams which directly express the contexts described at left above. Translate and refine the initial abstract diagrams into designed environments in such a way that the essence and clarity of the original diagram is retained in the designed environment.

	diagram	translation	solution
PLAN PATTERNS			
Diagram a 3 BR house whose principal rooms all face the same view.			
Diagram a 3 BR house arranged around an open courtyard.			
Diagram a 3 BR house arranged around an indoor space - living or family room.			

Conceive and draw diagrams which directly express the plan patterns described at left above. Translate and refine the initial abstract diagrams into designed environments in such a way that the essence and clarity of the original diagram is retained in the designed environment.

	diagram	translation	solution
Diagram a cluster arrangement for condominiums and suggest the focal points for the clusters.			
Diagram a 3 BR house which zones the adult areas of the house away from the children's areas.			
Diagram a 3 BR house which strongly separates daytime activities from nighttime activities.			

Conceive and draw diagrams which directly express the plan patterns described at left above. Translate and refine the initial abstract diagrams into designed environments in such a way that the essence and clarity of the original diagram is retained in the designed environment.

	diagram	translation	solution
SECTION PATTERNS			
Diagram the section of a 3 BR house that steps down a steep slope.			
Diagram the section of a 2 story house which clusters around a 2 story living room.			
Diagram a 2 story house in section which strongly separates sleeping from waking activities.			

Conceive and draw diagrams which directly express the section patterns described at left above. Translate and refine the initial abstract diagrams into designed environments in such a way that the essence and clarity of the original diagram is retained in the designed environment.

	diagram	translation	solution
Diagram the section of a building which combines offices, residences and shops, separating them vertically.			
Diagram the section of a 2 story, energy-efficient 3 BR house.			
Diagram the section of an airport with passenger arrival and pick-up on different levels.			

Conceive and draw diagrams which directly express the section patterns described at left above. Translate and refine the initial abstract diagrams into designed environments in such a way that the essence and clarity of the original diagram is retained in the designed environment.

REPRESENTATIONAL DRAWING

This section of the book is concerned with drawing's relationship to experience, and will be devoted exclusively to perspectives, since perspectives are the only design drawings that have a direct relationship to experience. While it may be true that the initial germ of a formal idea often occurs as a plan or section pattern, mature designers immediately represent the 3-dimensional quality of the idea to themselves in perspective sketches.

Unfortunately representational drawing often follows the practice of drafting which teaches perspective as a tedious, mechanically exact procedure which can only be accomplished after the plan and section are determined, and teaches shadow-casting as the projection of shadows from a fixed sun angle, rather than as a matter of placing the sun freely.

An opposite and equally unfortunate tendency is to teach representational drawing as art, pre-occupied with media and the drawing as an end in itself, rather than as a neutral representation of a designed environment.

PERCEPTION

Designers have traditionally been content to think of the drawing techniques with which they represent the environment in the categories inherited from art - based on media: pencil drawing; ink drawing, etc.

A much more useful way of thinking about drawing techniques, for an environmental designer, would be to classify them according to the way in which they represent the phenomena by which we perceive the environment. The chemical composition of a design drawing is of no importance, but how that drawing represents the surfaces and edges by which we perceive space might be very important.

A drawing technique might be chosen, then, for its appropriateness for studying or presenting certain qualities being sought in a designed environment. If the surfaces were all to be slick and characterless materials, for instance, there would be no point in choosing a drawing technique which demanded the rendering of all the surfaces. If, on the other hand, the environment were to have rich materials or needed strong shadows or subtle light distinctions, it would be necessary to render the surfaces.

SURFACE DRAWING

Our perception of space begins with the perception of a continuous background surface. Throughout our evolutionary history the earth's surface has always formed the lower half of our visual field, and it is only in relation to this continuous background surface that we are able to judge the size and distance of objects...... including potential friends and enemies.

One way of representing any environment in a drawing is to render all its surfaces -their respective tones and textures - as in a black and white photograph.

While this is the most realistic way of representing the world, it is extremely demanding in both time and skill. For many years such "surface" drawing was the traditional way of making architectural renderings, was uniquely appropriate for rendering the materials of that time, and provided a showcase for drawing skill. Surface drawing is demonstrated in the examples of technique which follow as TONE and TONE OF LINES.

EDGE DRAWING

The second characteristic of the environment to which our evolutionary history has led us to attend is its edges. Edges are of two kinds. The simpler kind of edge occurs where one surface intersects with another surface in such a way that both surfaces are visible.

The second kind of edge, however, is fundamentally different, and much more important for our evolutionary survival and for our kinesthetic experience of space: the edges which hide space. These are the edges from behind which our enemies have always appeared and behind which we can hide—those edges which move against their backgrounds when we move through the environment, progressively revealing or concealing more of the world, carrying the kinesthetic experience of space.

Simple line drawings can represent both kinds of edges, and if line drawings are profiled to make the distinction described above, they can be remarkably efficient representations of the environment. "Edge" drawing is demonstrated by the LINE drawings in the technique examples which follow.

DRAWING TECHNIQUES

This set of experiences is designed to help students try several different ways of representing environments by using various drawing techniques in their pure form. Unlike most classifications of drawing techniques, the ones which follow are not based on the media in which they are drawn, but according to the way they render the two characteristics of the environment by which we perceive space: surfaces and edges.

Although I have indicated what, for me, are the relative time and skill factors for each technique, experience alone will demonstrate which are the most easily mastered, and least time-consuming for each individual, so that future choices of drawing technique may be informed and intelligent. As in other matters, however, real freedom of choice will depend on your mastering several techniques. Most designers eventually develop their own individual combinations of the pure techniques.

LINE _____

- *spatial edges and planar corners defined with lines.*
- *surfaces unrendered.*

  time factor: 1
  skill factor: 1

LINE•SPATIALLY PROFILED _____

- *spatial edges and planar corners defined with lines.*
- *spatial edges profiled — the farther an edge lies in front of its background the heavier the line should be, except that its heaviness should be lightened in proportion to the distance it is away from the viewer.*
- *surfaces unrendered.*

  time factor: 1½
  skill factor: 1

TONE

- *surfaces toned evenly in relation to their differential reflectance of light.*
- *spatial edges and planar corners defined by a change in tone — no lines.*
- *stroking direction should respond to vertical or horizontal orientation of the surfaces, with the horizontal stroking always going toward the farthest vanishing point.*
- *surface tones may be graduated within the surface to heighten contrasts with other tones at the surface's edges.*

time factor: 10
skill factor: 10

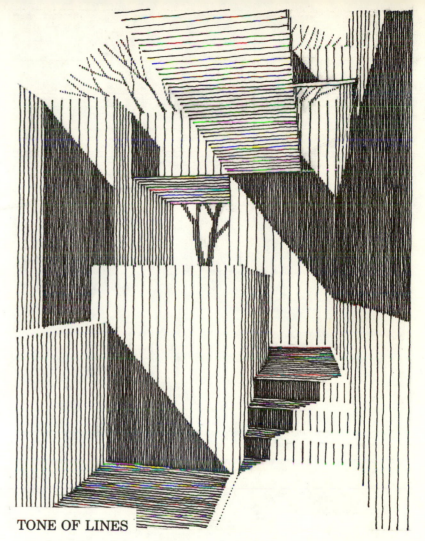

TONE OF LINES

- *surfaces toned in relation to their differential reflectance of light.*
- *tones made up of evenly spaced lines.*
- *spatial edges and planar corners defined by a change in line spacing — no spatial edge lines.*
- *direction of lines should respond to vertical or horizontal orientation of the surfaces, with horizontal lines always going toward the farthest vanishing point.*

time factor: 12
skill factor: 8

37

LINE AND TONE

- *spatial edges and planar corners defined with lines.*
- *spatial edges profiled — the farther an edge lies in front of its background the heavier the line should be, except that its heaviness should be lightened in proportion to the distance it is away from the viewer.*
- *surfaces toned evenly in relation to their differential reflectance of light.*
- *stroking direction should respond to vertical or horizontal orientation of the surfaces, with the horizontal stroking always going toward the farthest vanishing point.*

time factor: 8 and variable
skill factor: 4 and variable

38

LINE AND TONE
BLACK AND WHITE ON MIDDLETONE

- *spatial edges and planar corners defined with lines.*
- *spatial edges profiled — the farthest an edge lies in front of its background the heavier the line should be, except that its heaviness should be lightened in proportion to the distance it is away from the viewer.*
- *surfaces toned evenly in relation to their differential reflectance of light — black for shadow, white for sunlight, unrendered middletone paper for shade.*
- *stroking direction should respond to vertical or horizontal orientation of the surfaces, with the horizontal stroking always going toward the farthest vanishing point.*

time factor: 7 and variable
skill factor: 4 and variable

TONE OF LINES
BLACK AND WHITE ON MIDDLETONE

- *surfaces toned in relation to their differential reflectance of light.*
- *tones made up of evenly spaced lines — black for shadow, white for sunlight, unrendered middletone paper for shade.*
- *spatial edges and planar corners defined by a change in line spacing — no spatial edge lines.*
- *direction of lines should respond to vertical or horizontal orientation of the surfaces, with horizontal lines always going toward the farthest vanishing point.*

time factor: 11
skill factor: 8

TONE
BLACK AND WHITE ON MIDDLETONE

- *surfaces toned in relation to their differential reflectance of light — black for shadow, white for sunlight, unrendered middletone paper for shade.*
- *spatial edges and planar corners defined by a change in tone — no lines.*
- *stroking direction should respond to vertical or horizontal orientation of the surfaces, with horizontal stroking always going toward the farthest vanishing point.*

time factor: 9
skill factor: 10

39

Instructions for completing the drawing technique experiences which follow.

The four tracing paper sheets which follow each has a pair of drawings which will let you experience rendering the same drawing in two different techniques so you can experience the relative time and difficulty of the various techniques.

In each case the drawing on the left is printed very lightly and is to be rendered in TONE or TONE OF LINES so that the printed lines will serve only as guidelines and should disappear in the final drawing.

The right hand drawing in each case is intended to be spatially profiled and rendered in LINE AND TONE. Shadows (which will be covered under LIGHT page (65) are cast for you in order to make the finished drawings stronger.

The experiences are printed on tracing paper so the finished drawings may be blue-printed or Xeroxed onto middletone paper (see REPRODUCTION TECHNIQUES page 128) to further understand the opportunities or problems with the various reproduction techniques.

41

SPATIAL STRUCTURE

The representation of 3-dimensional space in a 2-dimensional drawing begins with establishing a measurable spatial structure which will become the environment being designed. In addition to locating the various surfaces and edges of the environment in perspective, such a spatial structure allows the projection and rendering of light in the environment. What is often taught under the separate titles of PERSPECTIVE and SHADOW-CASTING is better understood as being constituents of the same spatial structure.

If environmental designers are to know what the experience of the environments they are designing will be, they must master the drawing of the integrated spatial structure which allows them to represent 3-dimensional space in light.

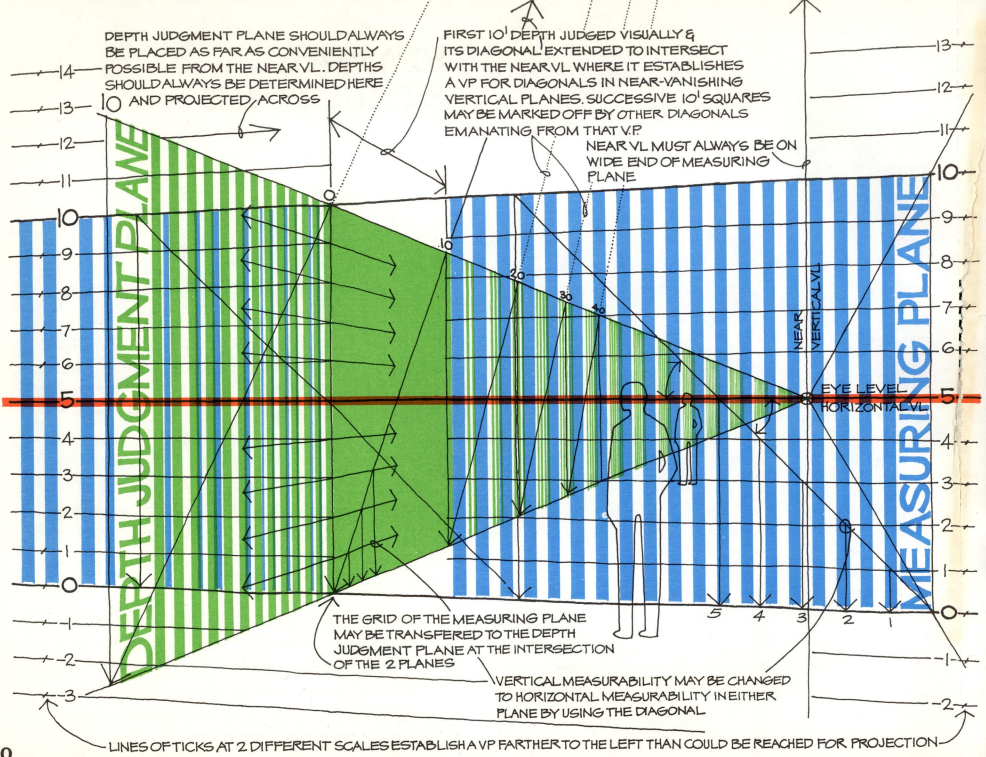

DEPTH JUDGMENT PLANE SHOULD ALWAYS BE PLACED AS FAR AS CONVENIENTLY POSSIBLE FROM THE NEAR VL. DEPTHS SHOULD ALWAYS BE DETERMINED HERE AND PROJECTED ACROSS

FIRST 10' DEPTH JUDGED VISUALLY & ITS DIAGONAL EXTENDED TO INTERSECT WITH THE NEAR VL WHERE IT ESTABLISHES A VP FOR DIAGONALS IN NEAR-VANISHING VERTICAL PLANES. SUCCESSIVE 10' SQUARES MAY BE MARKED OFF BY OTHER DIAGONALS EMANATING FROM THAT V.P.

NEAR VL MUST ALWAYS BE ON WIDE END OF MEASURING PLANE

DEPTH JUDGMENT PLANE

MEASURING PLANE

NEAR VERTICAL VL

EYE LEVEL
HORIZONTAL VL

THE GRID OF THE MEASURING PLANE MAY BE TRANSFERED TO THE DEPTH JUDGMENT PLANE AT THE INTERSECTION OF THE 2 PLANES

VERTICAL MEASURABILITY MAY BE CHANGED TO HORIZONTAL MEASURABILITY IN EITHER PLANE BY USING THE DIAGONAL

LINES OF TICKS AT 2 DIFFERENT SCALES ESTABLISH A VP FARTHER TO THE LEFT THAN COULD BE REACHED FOR PROJECTION

SPATIAL INTEREST

Spatial interest is the basic category of drawing interest..... as it also is of environmental interest. Spatial interest in drawings, as in the environment, is promised kinesthetic interest - the anticipated experience of spaces and vistas which are hidden or only partly seen, but which will become available as we move through the spaces.

The main source of spatial interest in drawing is the number and clear representation of these partially revealed objects and spaces..... created by placing objects in front of surfaces and other objects, and profiling the edges which obscure the hidden spaces. Follow the bouncing ball or the paper airplane.

PERSPECTIVE

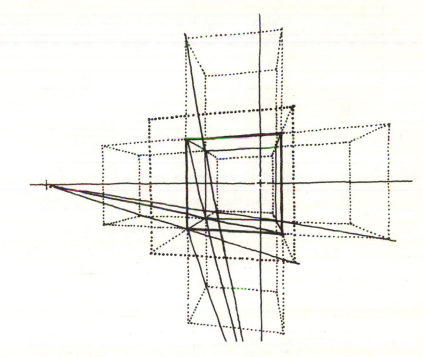

This set of experiences is designed to help students learn to structure 3-dimensional space directly and use perspective as a primary design drawing.

Traditional perspective methods are tedious and dependent on projection from a completed plan and section. This makes perspective a secondary drawing which can only be made after most of the design decisions have been reached. By using the simplified 2-line, 2-point method students can design directly in perspective.

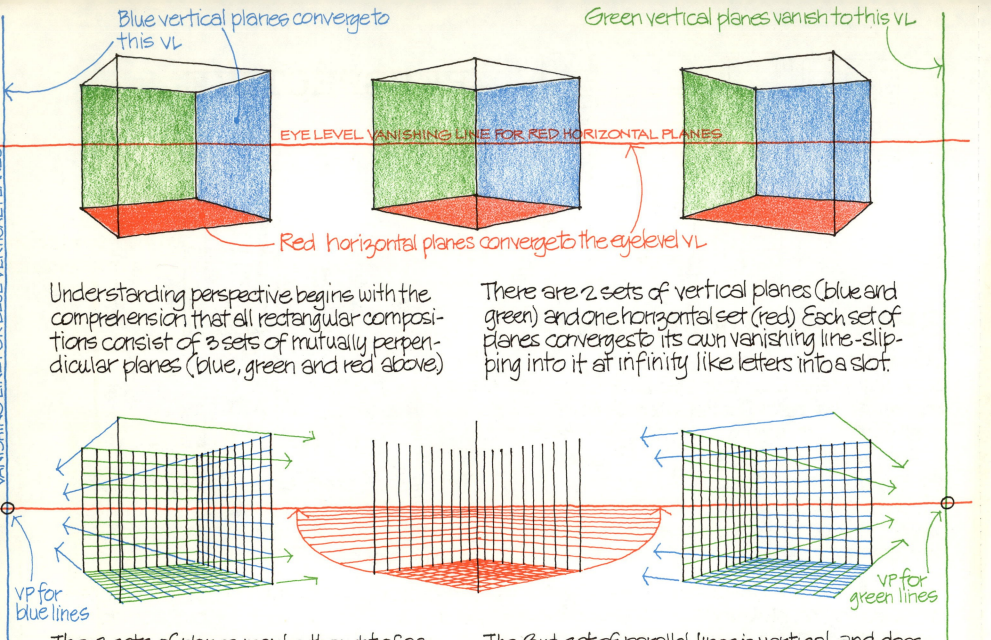

Blue vertical planes converge to this VL

Green vertical planes vanish to this VL

EYE LEVEL VANISHING LINE FOR RED HORIZONTAL PLANES

Red horizontal planes converge to the eye level VL

VANISHING LINE FOR BLUE VERTICAL PLANES

VP for blue lines

VP for green lines

Understanding perspective begins with the comprehension that all rectangular compositions consist of 3 sets of mutually perpendicular planes (blue, green and red above.)

There are 2 sets of vertical planes (blue and green) and one horizontal set (red.) Each set of planes converges to its own vanishing line - slipping into it at infinity like letters into a slot.

The 3 sets of planes may be thought of as consisting of perpendicular pairings of 3 sets of parallel lines. 2 of the pairs are horizontal lines (blue and green) and vanish toward a VP where the eye level VL intersects the blue or green VL.

The 3rd set of parallel lines is vertical and does not converge. The 2 sets of lines which make up the horizontal planes (red) may also be conceived of as rotating like the ribs of a woman's fan and collapsing into the eye level VL at infinity since their VPs are on that VL.

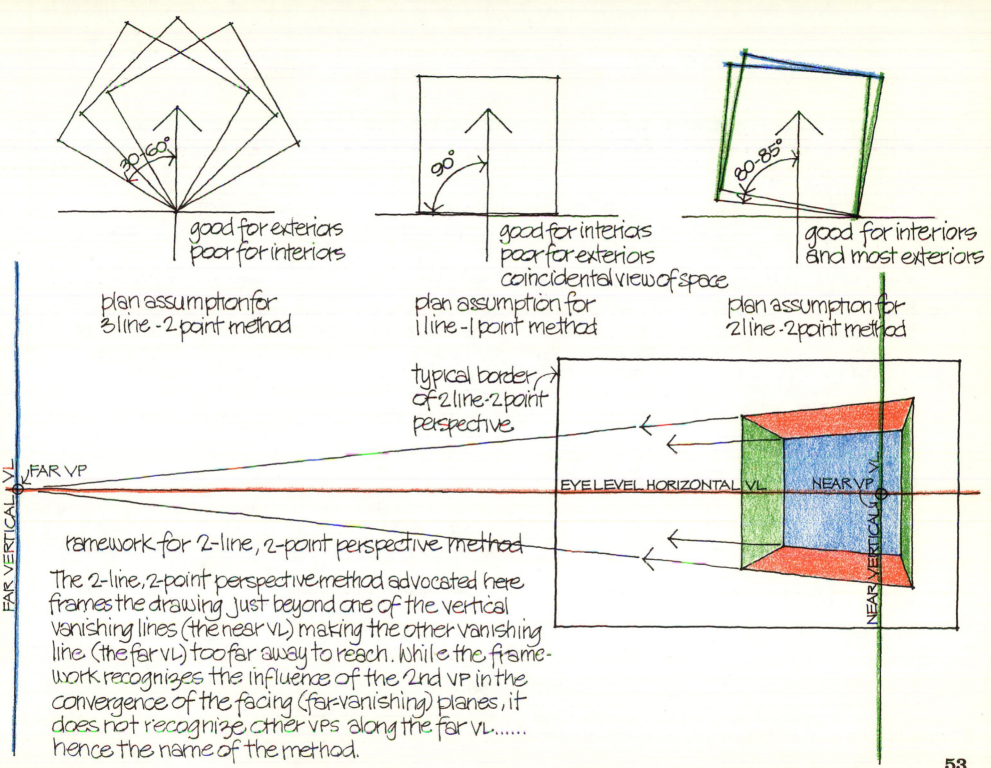

30°-60°

good for exteriors
poor for interiors

plan assumption for
3 line - 2 point method

90°

good for interiors
poor for exteriors
coincidental view of space

plan assumption for
1 line - 1 point method

80°-85°

good for interiors
and most exteriors

plan assumption for
2 line - 2 point method

typical border
of 2 line - 2 point
perspective

FAR VERTICAL VL

FAR VP

EYE LEVEL HORIZONTAL VL

NEAR VP

NEAR VERTICAL VL

framework for 2-line, 2-point perspective method

The 2-line, 2-point perspective method advocated here
frames the drawing just beyond one of the vertical
vanishing lines (the near VL) making the other vanishing
line (the far VL) too far away to reach. While the framework recognizes the influence of the 2nd VP in the
convergence of the facing (far-vanishing) planes, it
does not recognize other VPs along the far VL......
hence the name of the method.

53

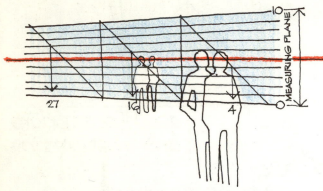

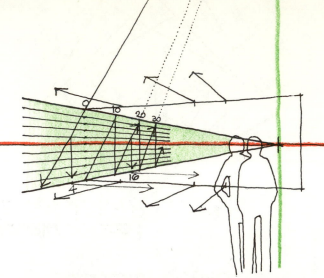

- MARK OFF VERTICAL & LATERAL MEASUREMENTS BY INTERSECTING THE GRID OF THE MEASURING PLANE WITH A 45° DIAGONAL.

PERSPECTIVE METHOD

- PLACE A NEAR-VANISHING DEPTH-JUDGMENT PLANE AS FAR AWAY FROM THE NEAR VP AS POSSIBLE.
- JUDGE A 10' DEPTH AND ESTABLISH THE VP FOR DIAGONALS IN NEAR-VANISHING VERTICAL PLANES.

- MARK OFF DEPTH MEASUREMENTS BY INTERSECTING THE CORNERED GRID WITH DIAGONALS FROM THE VP FOR VERTICAL DIAGONALS.
- EXTEND THE VERTICAL, LATERAL AND DEPTH MEASUREMENTS TO COMPLETE THE PERSPECTIVE.

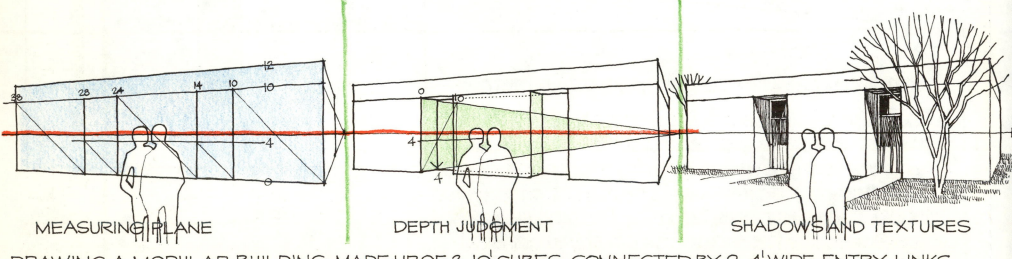

MEASURING PLANE   DEPTH JUDGMENT   SHADOWS AND TEXTURES

DRAWING A MODULAR BUILDING MADE UP OF 3 10' CUBES CONNECTED BY 2 4' WIDE ENTRY LINKS CONSISTING OF A 3' DOOR AND SIDELIGHT RECESSED 4' UNDER A 2' DEEP ROOF STRUCTURE

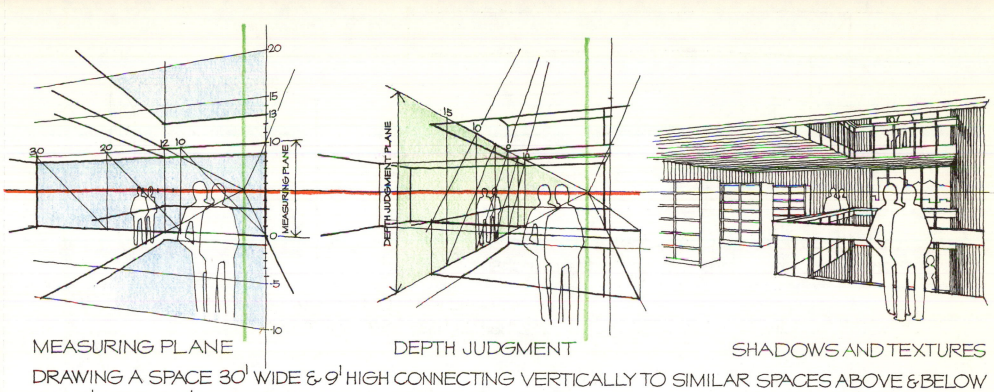

MEASURING PLANE   DEPTH JUDGMENT   SHADOWS AND TEXTURES

DRAWING A SPACE 30' WIDE & 9' HIGH CONNECTING VERTICALLY TO SIMILAR SPACES ABOVE & BELOW BY A 12' WIDE X 17' DEEP OPEN WELL SURROUNDED BY A 3' RAILING. WELL AT RIGHT SIDE OF THE SPACE

17

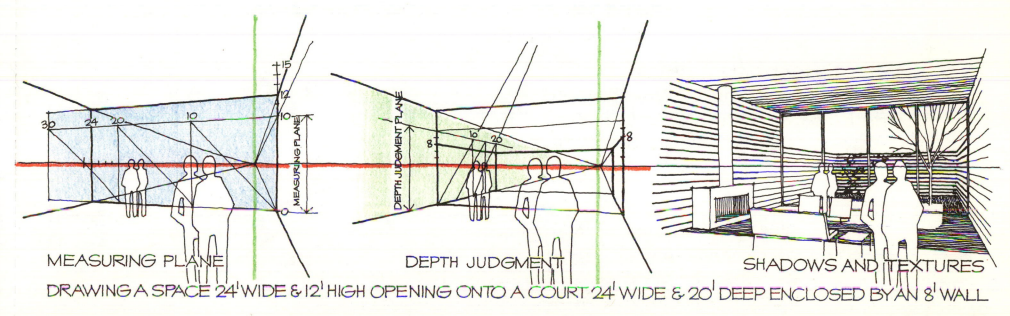

MEASURING PLANE   DEPTH JUDGMENT   SHADOWS AND TEXTURES

DRAWING A SPACE 24' WIDE & 12' HIGH OPENING ONTO A COURT 24' WIDE & 20' DEEP ENCLOSED BY AN 8' WALL

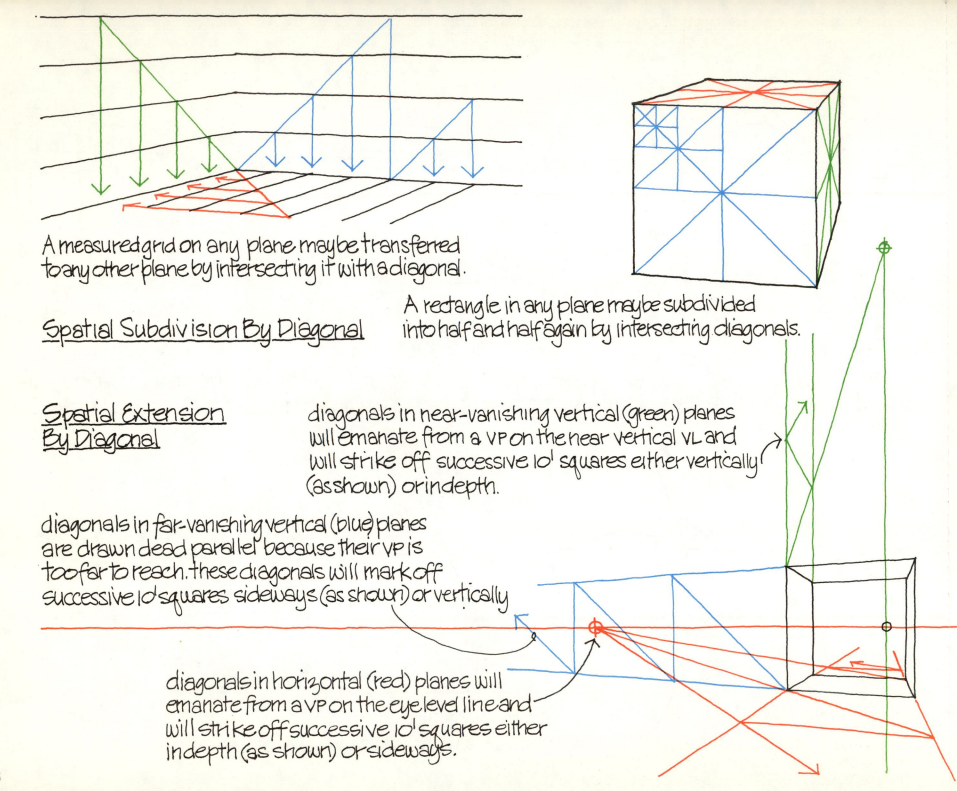

A measured grid on any plane may be transferred to any other plane by intersecting it with a diagonal.

Spatial Subdivision By Diagonal

A rectangle in any plane may be subdivided into half and half again by intersecting diagonals.

Spatial Extension By Diagonal

diagonals in near-vanishing vertical (green) planes will emanate from a VP on the near vertical VL and will strike off successive 10' squares either vertically (as shown) or in depth.

diagonals in far-vanishing vertical (blue) planes are drawn dead parallel because their VP is too far to reach. these diagonals will mark off successive 10' squares sideways (as shown) or vertically

diagonals in horizontal (red) planes will emanate from a VP on the eye level line and will strike off successive 10' squares either in depth (as shown) or sideways.

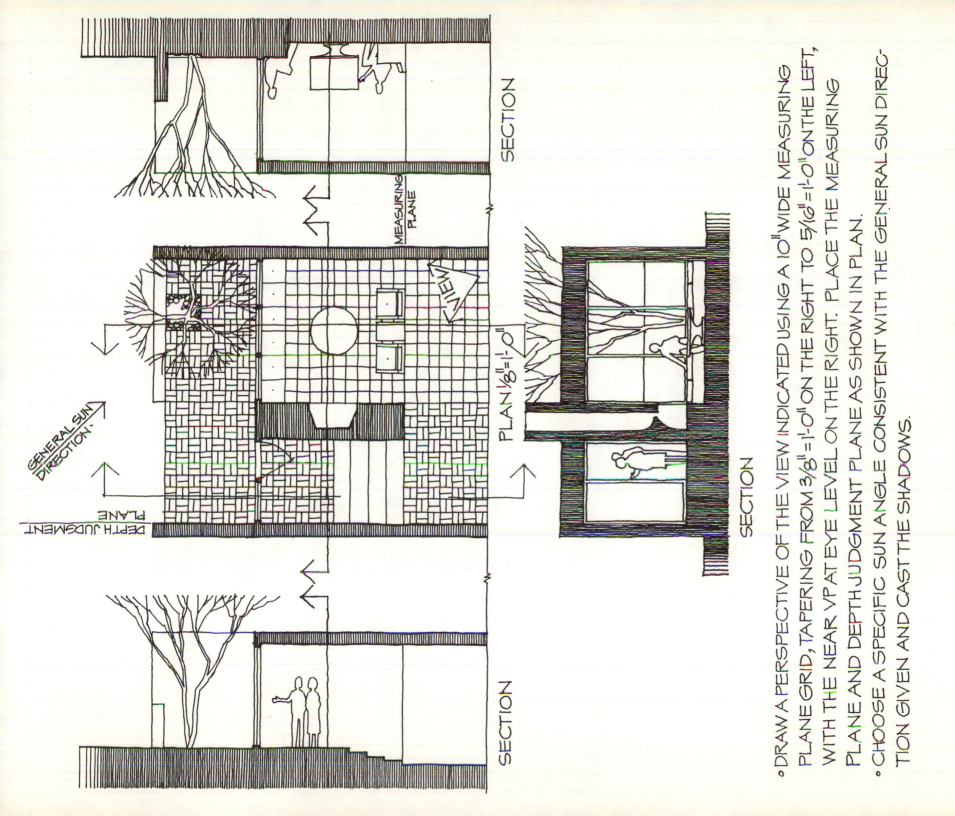

SECTION

SECTION

MEASURING PLANE

VIEW

GENERAL SUN DIRECTION

DEPTH JUDGMENT PLANE

PLAN 1/8"=1'-0"

SECTION

SECTION

° DRAW A PERSPECTIVE OF THE VIEW INDICATED USING A 10" WIDE MEASURING PLANE GRID, TAPERING FROM 3/8"=1'-0" ON THE RIGHT TO 5/16"=1'-0" ON THE LEFT, WITH THE NEAR VP AT EYE LEVEL ON THE RIGHT. PLACE THE MEASURING PLANE AND DEPTH JUDGMENT PLANE AS SHOWN IN PLAN.

° CHOOSE A SPECIFIC SUN ANGLE CONSISTENT WITH THE GENERAL SUN DIREC-TION GIVEN AND CAST THE SHADOWS.

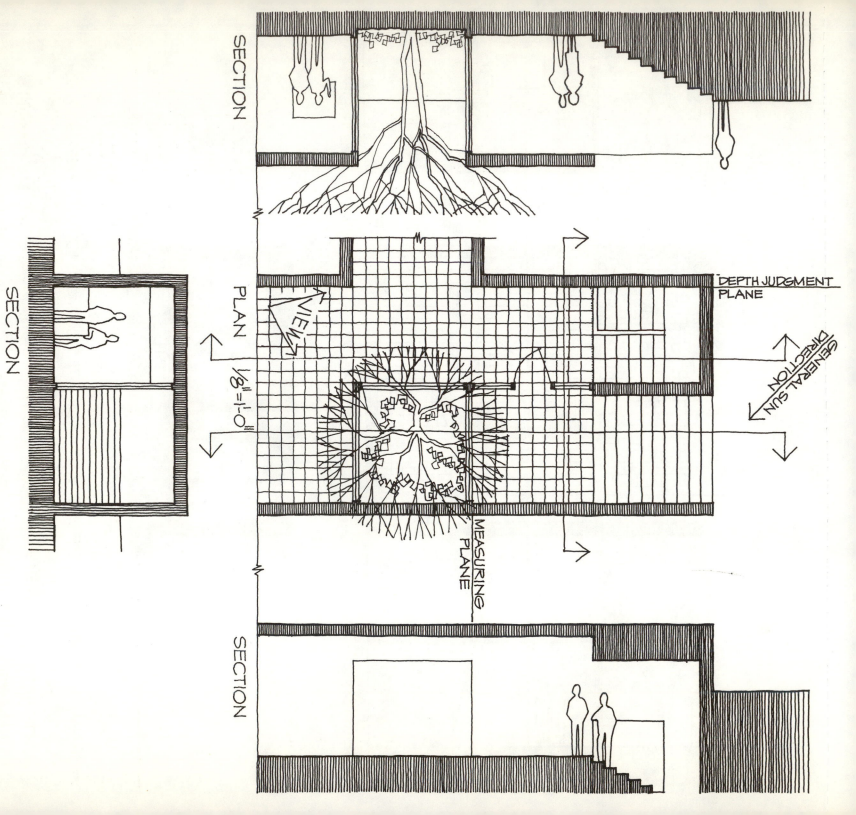

- DRAW A PERSPECTIVE USING A 10" WIDE MEASURING PLANE GRID, TAPERING FROM 3/8"=1'-0" ON THE LEFT TO 5/16"=1'-0" ON THE RIGHT, WITH THE NEAR VPON THE LEFT AT EYE LEVEL. PLACE THE MEASURING PLANE AND DEPTH JUDG-MENT PLANE WHERE THEY ARE SHOWN IN PLAN.
- CHOOSE A SPECIFIC SUN ANGLE CONSISTENT WITH THE GENERAL SUN DIREC-TION GIVEN AND CAST THE SHADOWS.

SECTION

SECTION

PLAN ⅛"=1'-0"

VIEW

DEPTH JUDGMENT PLANE

GENERAL SUN DIRECTION

MEASURING PLANE

SECTION

58

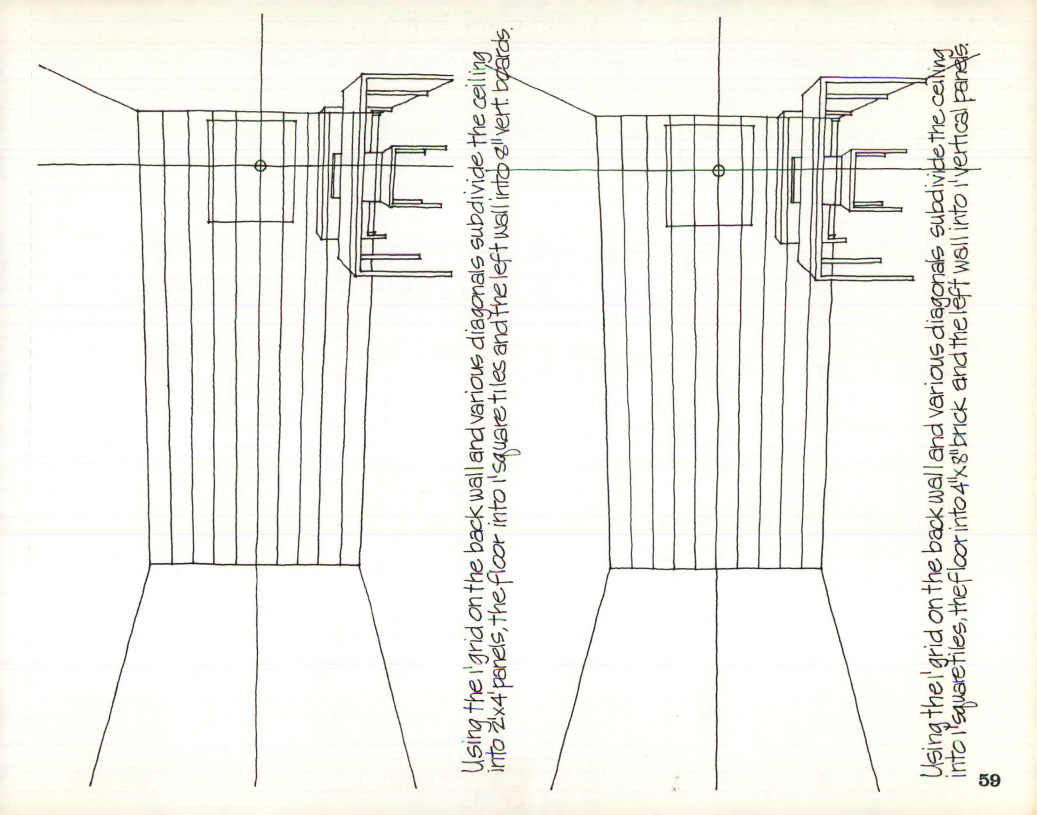

Using the 1' grid on the back wall and various diagonals subdivide the ceiling into 2'x4' panels, the floor into 1' square tiles and the left wall into 9" vert. boards.

Using the 1' grid on the back wall and various diagonals subdivide the ceiling into 1' square tiles, the floor into 4"x8" brick and the left wall into 1' vertical panels.

59

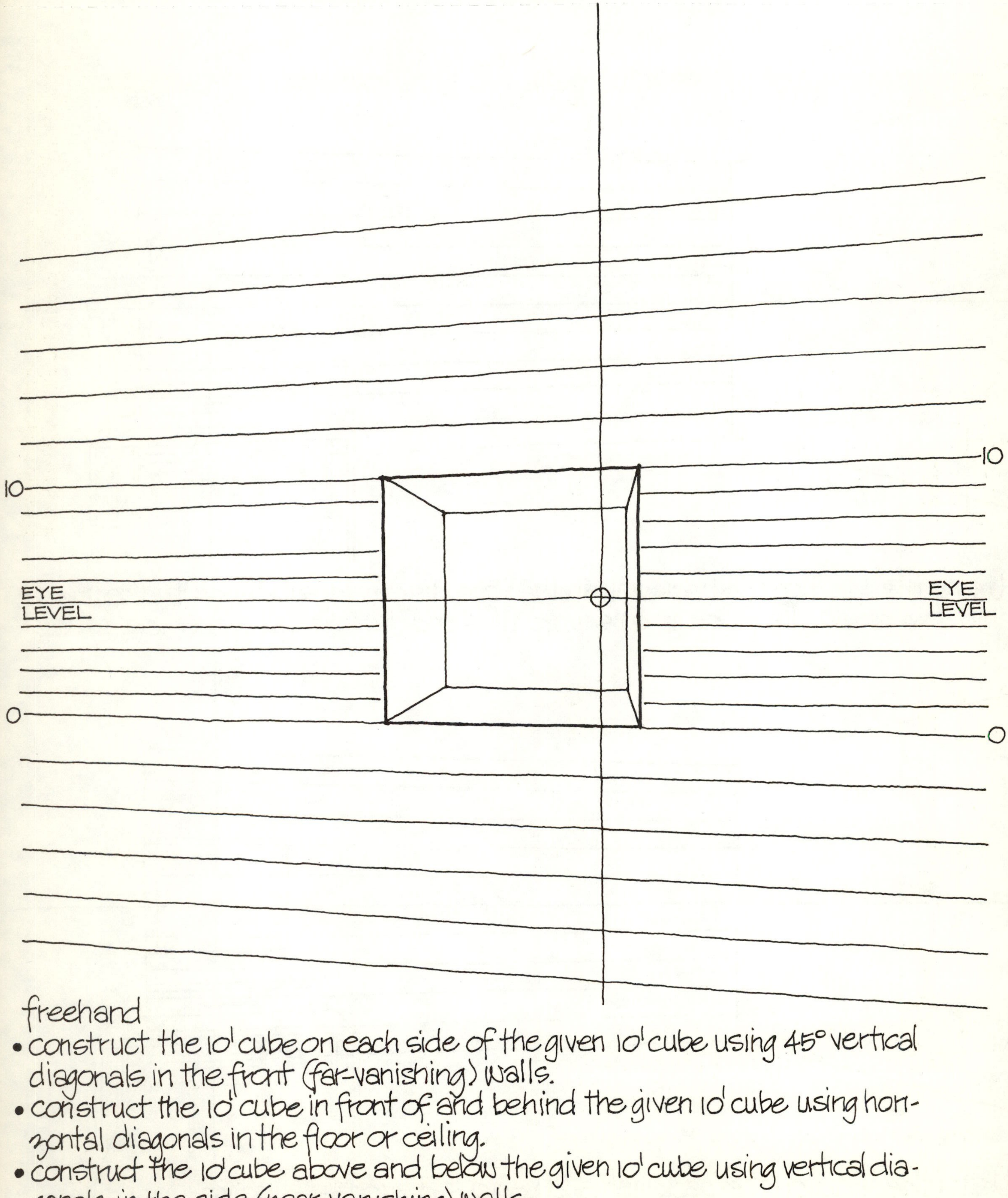

freehand
- construct the 10' cube on each side of the given 10' cube using 45° vertical diagonals in the front (far-vanishing) walls.
- construct the 10' cube in front of and behind the given 10' cube using horizontal diagonals in the floor or ceiling.
- construct the 10' cube above and below the given 10' cube using vertical diagonals in the side (near-vanishing) walls.
- draw a figure @ 5' eye level standing in the center of each cube.
- leave diagonals in pencil, ink the edges of each cube.

EYE LEVEL

10

EYE LEVEL

10

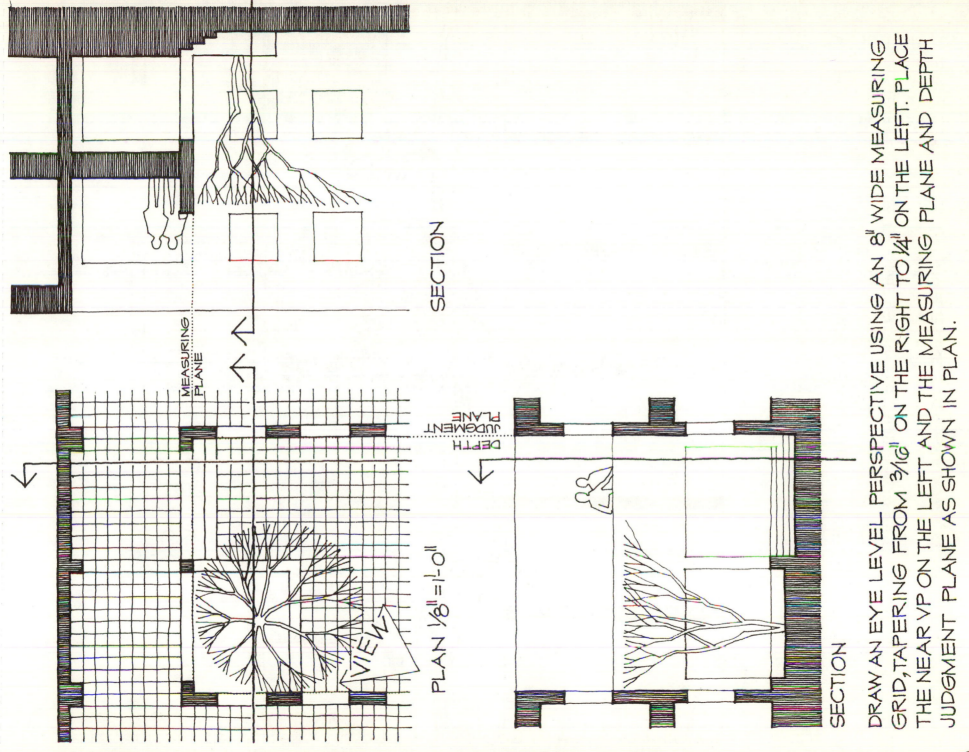

SECTION

MEASURING PLANE

PLAN ⅛" = 1'-0"

VIEW

DEPTH JUDGEMENT PLANE

SECTION

DRAW AN EYE LEVEL PERSPECTIVE USING AN 8" WIDE MEASURING GRID, TAPERING FROM ³⁄₁₆" ON THE RIGHT TO ¼" ON THE LEFT. PLACE THE NEAR VP ON THE LEFT AND THE MEASURING PLANE AND DEPTH JUDGMENT PLANE AS SHOWN IN PLAN.

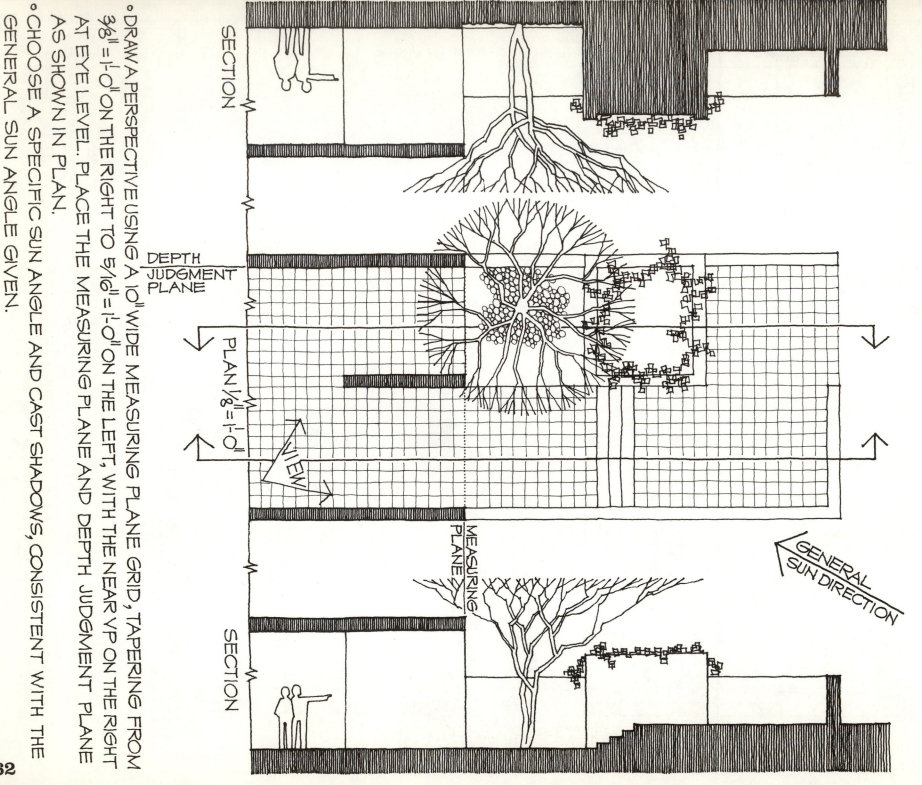

SECTION

DEPTH
JUDGMENT
PLANE

PLAN 1/8" = 1'-0"

VIEW

MEASURING PLANE

SECTION

GENERAL SUN DIRECTION

- DRAW A PERSPECTIVE USING A 10" WIDE MEASURING PLANE GRID, TAPERING FROM 3/8" = 1'-0" ON THE RIGHT TO 5/16" = 1'-0" ON THE LEFT, WITH THE NEAR VP ON THE RIGHT AT EYE LEVEL. PLACE THE MEASURING PLANE AND DEPTH JUDGMENT PLANE AS SHOWN IN PLAN.
- CHOOSE A SPECIFIC SUN ANGLE AND CAST SHADOWS, CONSISTENT WITH THE GENERAL SUN ANGLE GIVEN.

62

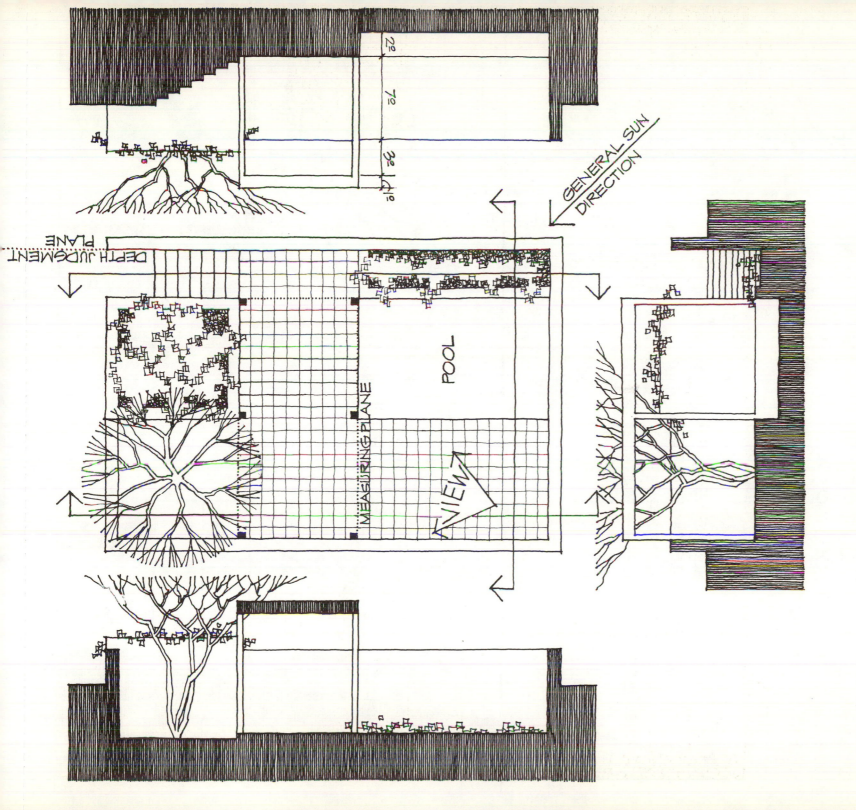

CONSTRUCT AN EYE LEVEL PERSPECTIVE OF THIS SUNKEN GARDEN FROM THE INDICATED VIEW DIRECTION USING A 3/8" X 5/16" X 10" MEASURING GRID. CAST THE SHADOWS AND INDICATE THE SHADE WITH SUN COMING FROM THE QUADRANT SHOWN.

GENERAL SUN DIRECTION

DEPTH JUDGMENT PLANE

MEASURING PLANE

POOL

VIEW

63

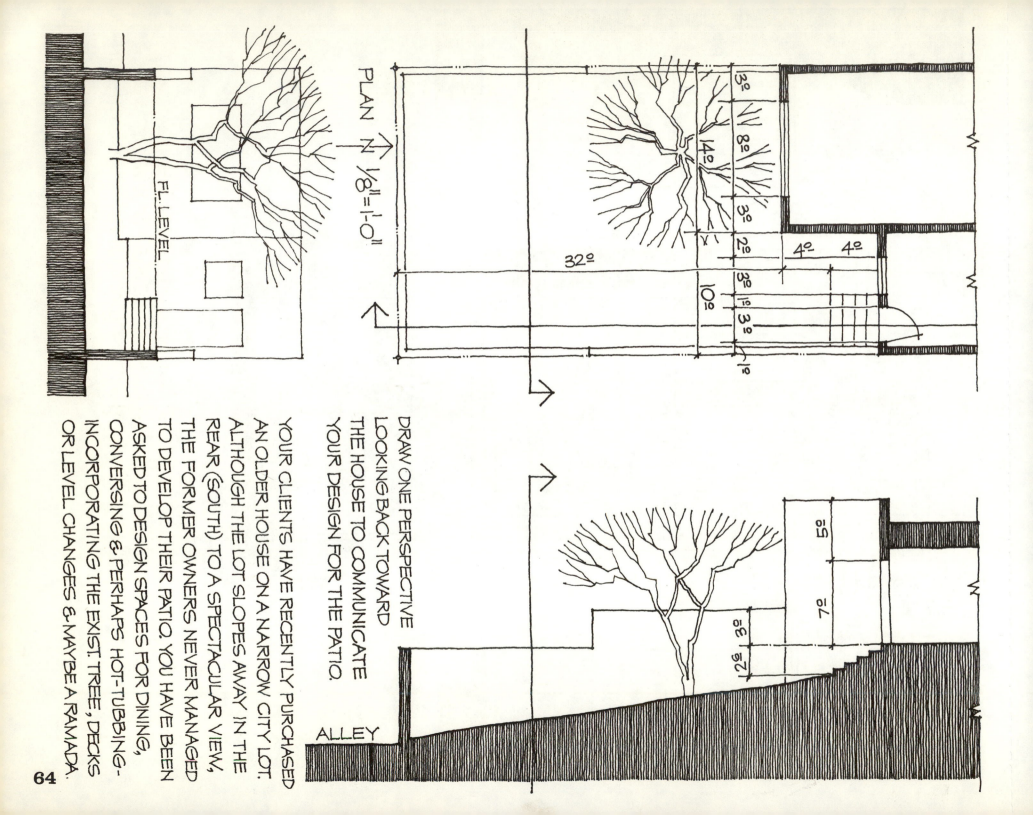

PLAN N 1/8"=1'-0"

FL. LEVEL

32° 3° 8° 14° 3° 2° 4° 4° 3° 1° 3° 10° 1°

5° 7° 3° 7°

ALLEY

DRAW ONE PERSPECTIVE LOOKING BACK TOWARD THE HOUSE TO COMMUNICATE YOUR DESIGN FOR THE PATIO.

YOUR CLIENTS HAVE RECENTLY PURCHASED AN OLDER HOUSE ON A NARROW CITY LOT. ALTHOUGH THE LOT SLOPES AWAY IN THE REAR (SOUTH) TO A SPECTACULAR VIEW, THE FORMER OWNERS NEVER MANAGED TO DEVELOP THEIR PATIO. YOU HAVE BEEN ASKED TO DESIGN SPACES FOR DINING, CONVERSING & PERHAPS HOT-TUBBING-INCORPORATING THE EXIST. TREE, DECKS OR LEVEL CHANGES & MAYBE A RAMADA.

LIGHT

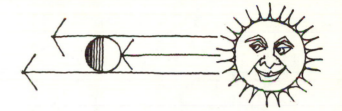

TONAL INTEREST

Tonal interest is the most powerful of the interest categories - the last to be squinted out, and the one which can be seen from the greatest distance. Tonal interest depends on using the full range of grays, from pure white to solid black over broad areas of the drawing.

The main source of tonal interest is light, shade and shadow. The inherent color and therefore the darkness or lightness of materials is another source of tonal interest, but better ignored, especially in black and white drawings, in favor of rendering the material's texture.

This set of experiences is designed to help students study alternative shadow patterns on the environments they are designing and render them in various techniques. The tonal interest contributed by light, shade and shadow is potentially very time-consuming to add to a drawing, but is open to several short cuts which will be explored.

Shadow-casting is traditionally taught on plans, sections and elevations from a fixed sun angle. It is much more useful to learn shadow-casting whole, in 3-dimensions and to experience the freedom of studying and choosing the most characteristic or dramatic shadow patterns.

⊥ shadows of vertical lines on horiz. planes emanate from a VP on the VL for the planes on which they lie.

⊥ shadows of near-vanishing horiz. lines on far-vanishing vert. planes do not converge but are drawn dead parallel.

⊥ shadows of far-vanishing horizontal lines on near-vanishing vertical planes emanate from a VP on the VL for the planes on which they lie.

definitions - 3 light conditions

<u>sun</u> - a surface turned toward and lit by the sun.
<u>shade</u> - a surface turned away from the sun.
<u>shadow</u> - an area turned toward the sun but unlit because of an intervening mass.
shade and shadow always occur together in interdependent shade/shadow systems

<u>casting edge</u> - any outside corner that separates sun from shade

<u>projected shade/shadow system</u>
casting edge 01234 casts shadow
$0 1_s 2_s 3_s 4$

all shade/shadow systems begin with perpendicular shadows

<u>indented shade/shadow system</u>
casting edge ABC casts shadow
$A B_s C$

shadows always alternate from ⊥ to ‖ to ⊥ when they change planes

<u>step shade/shadow system</u>
casting edge XYZ casts shadow
$X Y_s Z$

2
2_s
3_s
1_s
4
×0
A
B_s
B
C
Y_s
Y
Z

Each set of perpendicular shadows has its own VP on the VL for the planes on which the shadows lie.

Perpendicular Relationship
(horiz. pole to blue surfaces) perpendicular shadows vary dramatically in both length and angle but at any moment are parallel to one another.

Parallel Relationship
(horiz. pole to red surfaces) parallel shadows are always parallel to the line which casts them.

A

Parallel shadows always converge to the appropriate VP of the perspective or remain vertical if cast by vertical lines.

Shadows always begin with a ⊥ shadow and then alternate between ⊥ and ‖ as they change planes because the 2nd plane will always be ⊥ to the first.

This open cube represents all 3 ⊥ shadow-casting relationships and, in the coincidental view above, eliminates all the parallel shadows so the 3 ⊥ shadows and their 2 VPs. may be seen clearly.

Free shadow-casting begins with choosing the angles of 2 of the 3 ⊥ shadows.

You will learn a great deal about shadow-casting by building a cube like the one above and taking it out in the sunlight.

In rectangular compositions there are only 2 possible relationships between any line which casts a shadow and the plane on which the line's shadow falls: perpendicular ⊥ or parallel ‖.

- Free shadow-casting begins with choosing the general direction of the sun (in this example in front of and to the right of the viewer).

- Next make a sun/shade analysis to determine which surfaces will be in sun and which in shade.

- Render the surfaces in shade and identify the casting edges (outside corners which separate sun and shade) including those which are hidden.

- Notice that with the sun assumption in this example all the far-vanishing planes (blue) are in shade. This means that there will only be 2 ⊥ shadows to deal with and both may be chosen freely, and independently of one another, because the remaining ⊥ shadows will fall on the sunlit backs of the far-vanishing (blue) vertical planes which can't be seen in this view.

- The shade/shadow systems will all begin at points where a casting edge intersects a sunlit plane.

- The shadows which emanate from such points will all be perpendicular shadows and the choice of their angles will determine the over-all shadow pattern.

- There are 7 such points in this example.

- Identify the most prominent or most frequently occuring ⊥ shadow angle (in this example it is the shadows of far-vanishing horizontal lines on near-vanishing (green) vertical planes - 4 of 7).

- Assume the most beneficial angle for this set of ⊥ shadows and establish its VP on the VL for the planes on which the shadows lie.

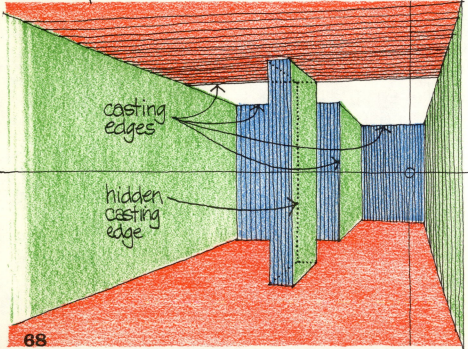

casting edges

hidden casting edge

68

this shadow could fall anywhere within this quadrant.

It seems most critical since where it hits the floor and comes across the floor will form a good base for the dwg.

1 2 3 4

A B C

- Extend this set of ⊥ shadows from its vp at all 4 of the initial points of the shade/shadow systems, following the rules for alternating ⊥ and ‖ shadows on perpendicular planes (page 67) until the shadows reach a surface in shade.

- This is the maximum length of these shadows. They will be intersected by the extension of ⊥ shadows coming from the other end of each shade/shadow system.

- They could be intersected before they even get off of the green planes by ‖ shadows extending up the walls (see the alternate shown in the next step).

Finally we choose an angle for the other set of ⊥ shadows (the shadows of vertical lines on horizontal [red] planes.) We may choose this angle anywhere within the quadrant shown - independent of the preceding ⊥ shadow angle. The greatest opportunity in this choice seems to be the placement of the shadow of point A where it shows.

With the angle chosen the vp for the entire set may be found on the vL for the planes on which the shadows lie. The other ⊥ shadows of the set may then be extended from the vp to close the shade/shadow systems initiated in the previous steps.

Once the shadow pattern is completed and all the relationships established it is easy to vary the pattern to integrate it with the placement of figures, trees and furniture.

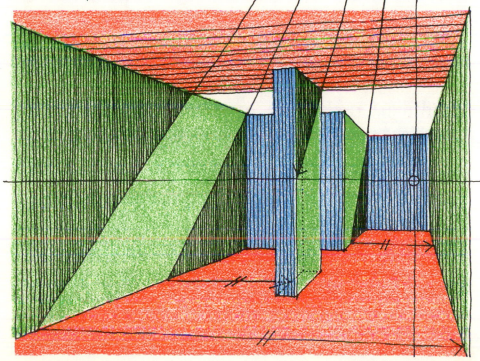

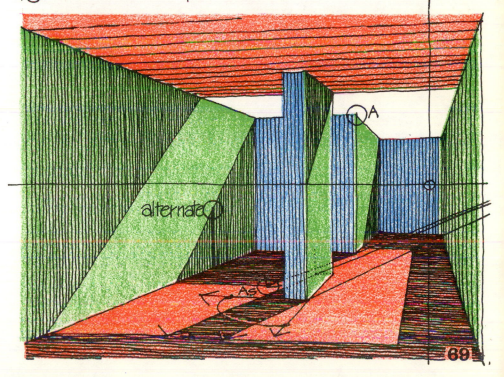

alternate

A

As

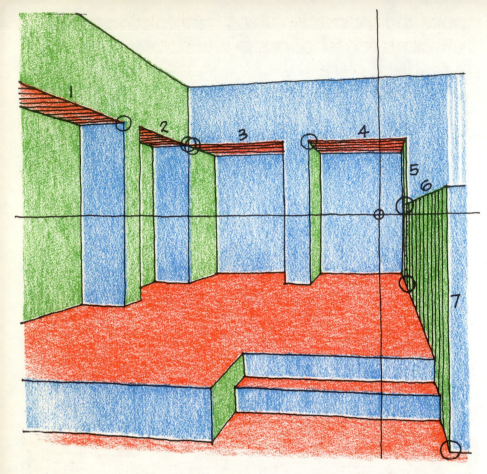

In this example the sun is assumed to be behind and to the right of the viewer, so that we will see all 3 sets of sunlit planes and the perpendicular shadows on them.

A sun/shade analysis reveals 7 casting edges, 2 of which (5 and 6) must be extended to reach a perpendicular sunlit plane on which to in-itiate a shade/shadow system. With the establish-ment of those 2 points we also have a total of 7 points from which ⊥ shadows will begin shade/ shadow systems.

There is no clear reason to begin with one or another of the ⊥ angles but it will probably be more inter-esting to let the sun reach the back walls of the 2 niches facing us.

So we might begin by the ⊥ angle shown (the shadows of far-vanishing horizontal lines on near-vanishing vertical planes) and establishing its VP on the VL for the planes in which the shadows lie......then extend the other ⊥ shadow from the same point

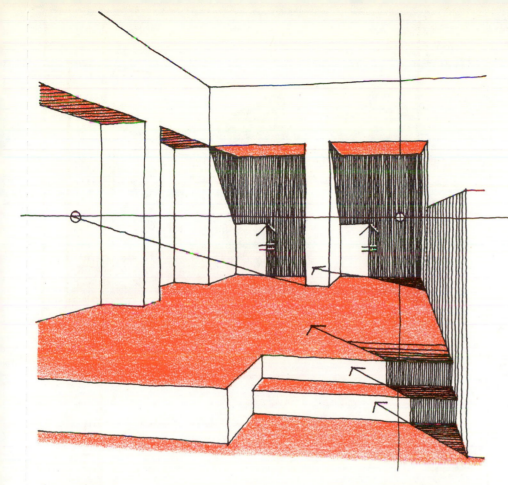

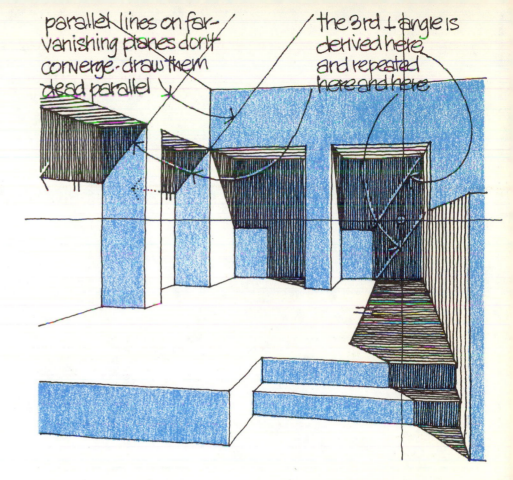

parallel lines on far-vanishing planes don't converge-draw them dead parallel

the 3rd ⊥ angle is derived here and repeated here and here

A second ⊥ shadow angle may be chosen freely, and independently from the previous choice, and here it seems that we need a strong floor shadow without completely filling up the facing niches with shadows.

So, we choose one in the left hand niche, extend the choice to establish a vp on the vl for horizontal planes, and then cast the floor shadow in the other niche and initiate the shade/shadow system up the stairs.

Having freely chosen 2 of the 3 ⊥ shadow angles we must now derive the 3rd angle, since it is not a matter of choice but was determined by the 2 previous choices.

In this example this 3rd ⊥ angle is the shadow of near-vanishing horizontal lines on far-vanishing vertical planes. This angle is special in that it's vp would be too far away to reach for projection so these shadows are drawn dead parallel.

71

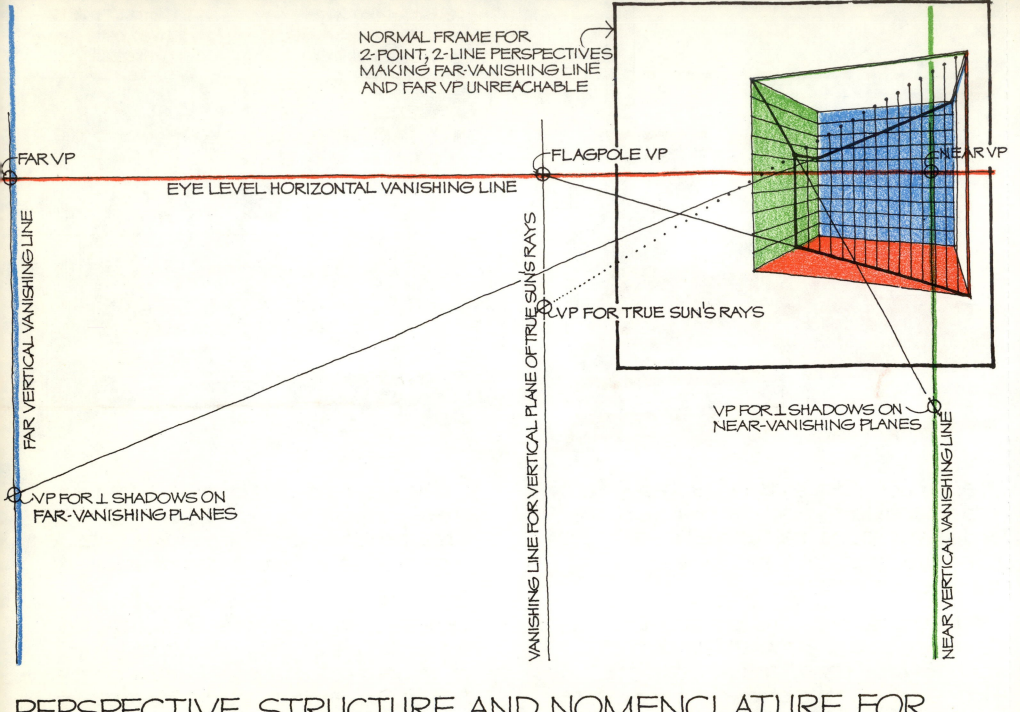

NORMAL FRAME FOR
2-POINT, 2-LINE PERSPECTIVES
MAKING FAR-VANISHING LINE
AND FAR VP UNREACHABLE

FAR VP

FLAGPOLE VP

NEAR VP

EYE LEVEL HORIZONTAL VANISHING LINE

FAR VERTICAL VANISHING LINE

VANISHING LINE FOR VERTICAL PLANE OF TRUE SUN'S RAYS

VP FOR TRUE SUN'S RAYS

VP FOR ⊥ SHADOWS ON
NEAR-VANISHING PLANES

VP FOR ⊥ SHADOWS ON
FAR-VANISHING PLANES

NEAR VERTICAL VANISHING LINE

PERSPECTIVE STRUCTURE AND NOMENCLATURE FOR
ORTHOGONAL SHADOW-CASTING RELATIONSHIPS

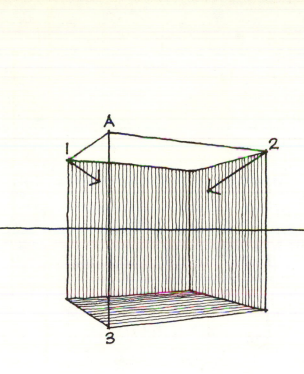

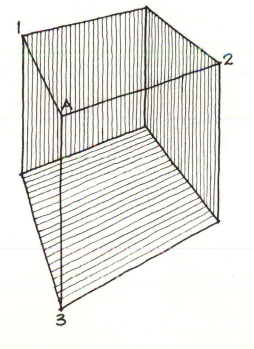

In the top cube
- find the shadow pattern cast by lines A1, A2 & A3 on the walls and floor of the cube when the shadows of lines A1 & A2 begin as shown.

In the bottom cube
- use the vps established for the shadow pattern of the top cube to draw the shadow pattern in the bottom cube.

In both cubes
- mark each piece of the shadow pattern with its relationship to the line which casts it. ($\perp$ or $\parallel$)
- color line A1, its $\perp$ shadow, the plane on which it falls and the VL for its $\perp$ shadow blue.
- color line A2, etc. green.
- color line A3, etc. red.
- color the vertical plane in which the true sun's rays lie violet.

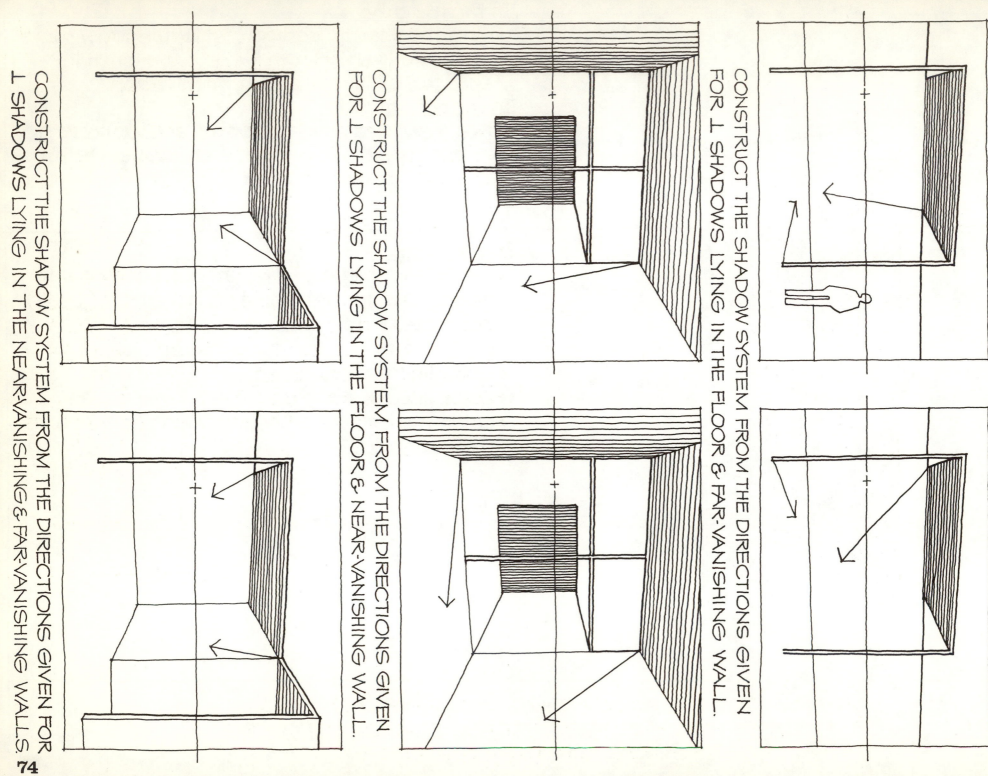

CONSTRUCT THE SHADOW SYSTEM FROM THE DIRECTIONS GIVEN FOR ⊥ SHADOWS LYING IN THE FLOOR & FAR-VANISHING WALL.

CONSTRUCT THE SHADOW SYSTEM FROM THE DIRECTIONS GIVEN FOR ⊥ SHADOWS LYING IN THE FLOOR & NEAR-VANISHING WALL.

CONSTRUCT THE SHADOW SYSTEM FROM THE DIRECTIONS GIVEN FOR ⊥ SHADOWS LYING IN THE NEAR-VANISHING & FAR-VANISHING WALLS.

74

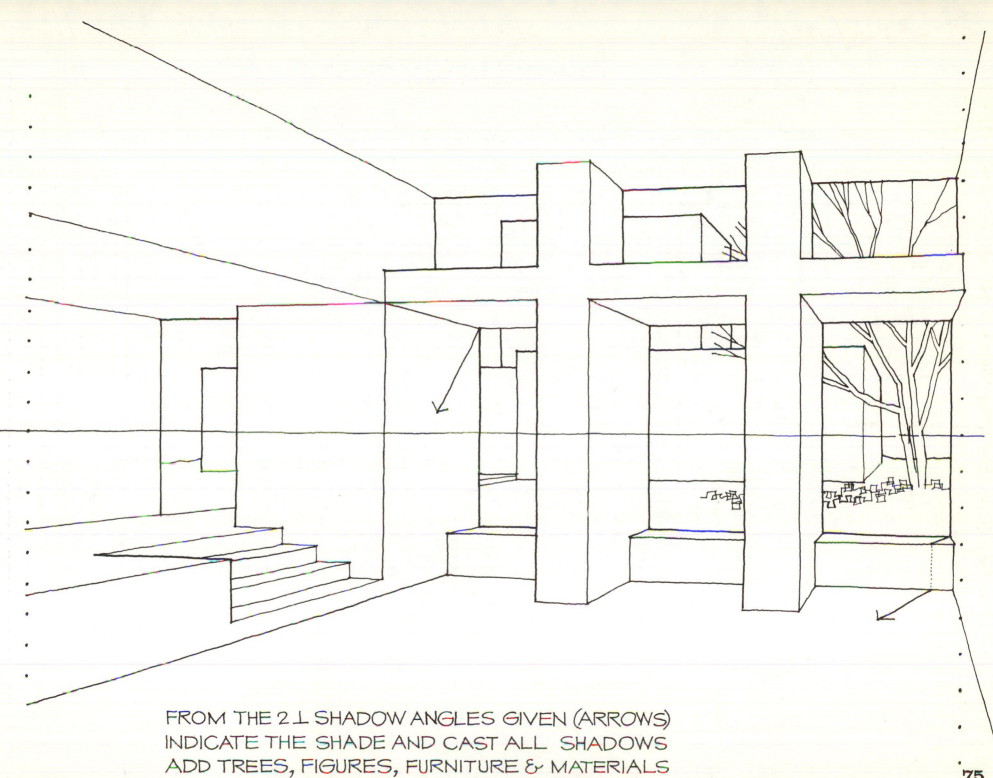

FROM THE 2 ⊥ SHADOW ANGLES GIVEN (ARROWS)
INDICATE THE SHADE AND CAST ALL SHADOWS
ADD TREES, FIGURES, FURNITURE & MATERIALS

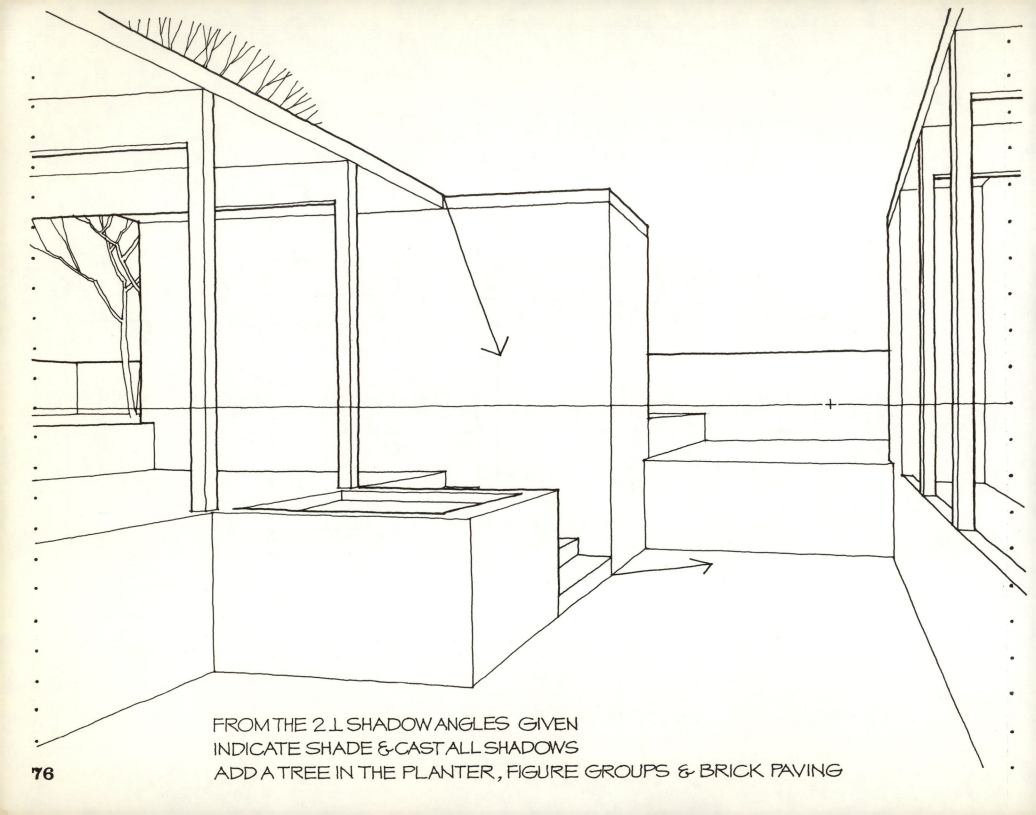

FROM THE 2 ⊥ SHADOW ANGLES GIVEN
INDICATE SHADE & CAST ALL SHADOWS
ADD A TREE IN THE PLANTER, FIGURE GROUPS & BRICK PAVING

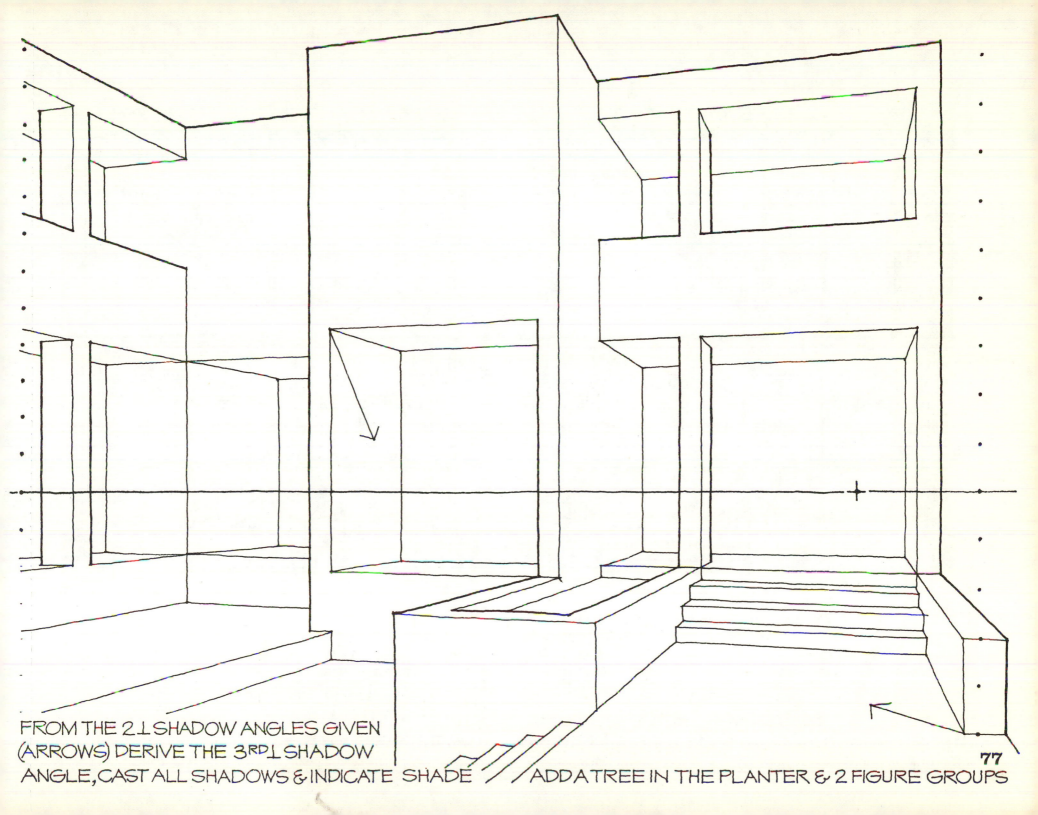

FROM THE 2 ⊥ SHADOW ANGLES GIVEN
(ARROWS) DERIVE THE 3ᴿᴰ ⊥ SHADOW
ANGLE, CAST ALL SHADOWS & INDICATE SHADE   ADD A TREE IN THE PLANTER & 2 FIGURE GROUPS

77

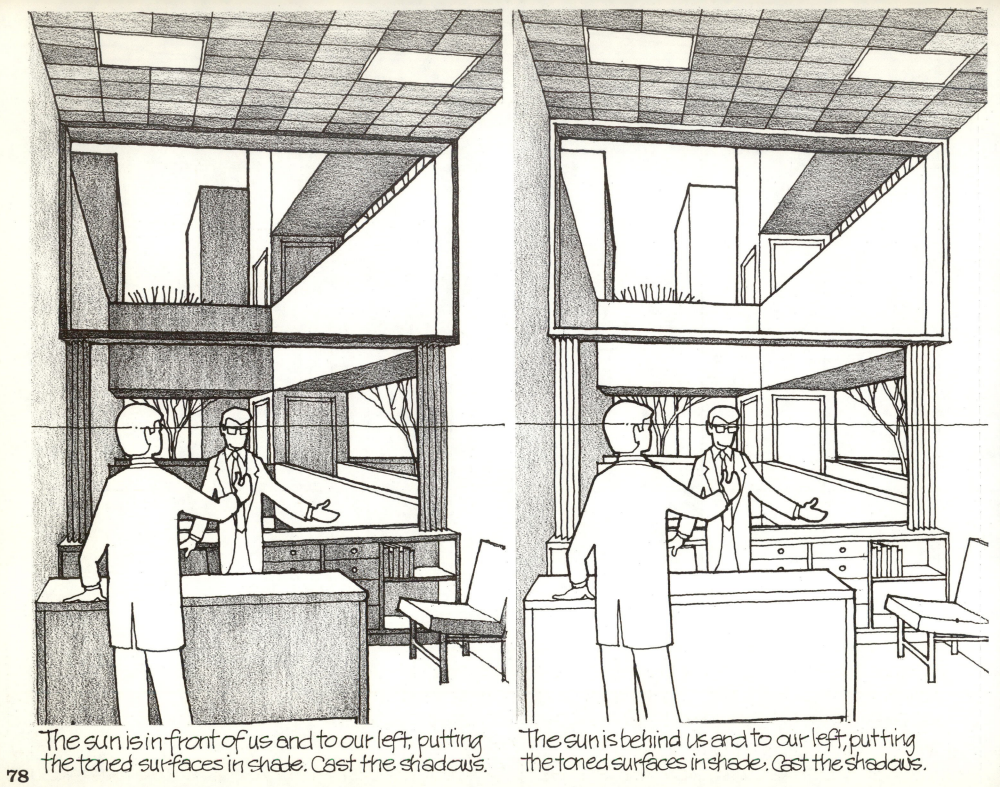

The sun is in front of us and to our left, putting the toned surfaces in shade. Cast the shadows.

The sun is behind us and to our left, putting the toned surfaces in shade. Cast the shadows.

DISREGARDING REFLECTIONS IN THE GLASS,
RENDER ALL THE SURFACES (INCLUDING FURNITURE) WITH PENCIL TONES AS THEY WOULD BE
ILLUMINATED IN INDIRECT LIGHT - NO SHADOWS. ASSUME WE ARE FACING SOUTH ON A CLOUDY
AFTERNOON, SO THAT THE LIGHT IS COMING FROM IN FRONT OF US AND TO OUR RIGHT. THE FIVE
VISIBLE SURFACE ORIENTATIONS WOULD THEN BE LIGHTED FROM 1 (LIGHTEST) TO 5 (DARKEST.)
1. UPWARD-FACING 2. WEST-FACING 3. EAST-FACING 4. DOWN-FACING 5. NORTH-FACING.

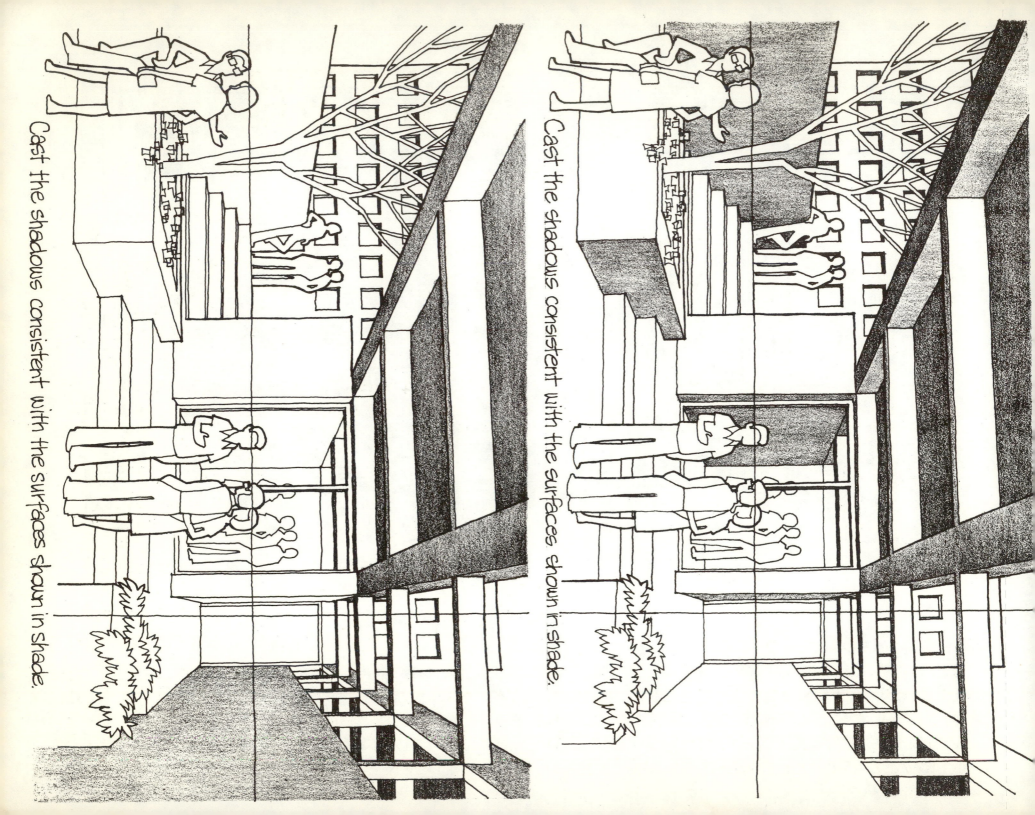

Cast the shadows consistent with the surfaces shown in shade.

Cast the shadows consistent with the surfaces shown in shade.

PERCEPTUAL TEMPLATES

Beyond drawing the spatial structure of an environment, representational drawing consists almost entirely of adding the textural interest of materials and the additional interest of figures, trees, plants and furniture. The ability to draw this collection of stuff is best thought of as the making and storing of perceptual templates which combine the criteria and controls necessary to draw the particular texture, figure, tree or chair. Another, perhaps more accurate, analogy for this kind of drawing is the prerecording and storage of videotapes in a memory bank.

These stored templates or tapes should come in a hierarchy based on distance from the viewer, level of detail and time and skill required; and the most valuable templates are those which are time-flexible, in that they become graphically acceptable very quickly, but are capable of additional refinement when the time becomes available.

81

TEXTURAL
INTEREST

Textural interest in drawing is anticipated tactile interest. The drawing tells us what certain surfaces will feel like. This is the most intimate of the interest categories and the best example of how the past experience of the other senses comes to reside in the visual sense.

The main source - virtually the only source of textural interest lies in the selection of materials.

MATERIALS

This set of experiences is designed to help students learn to render the specific materials of which their designs may be constructed. The materials of which an object or space is made must be appropriate to the form and to the construction process. The visual and physical properties of an environment's materials are inseparable from the functional or sensory experience of that environment. A designer should learn to draw and think of materials realistically.

Material selection and indication are very important in design and in design drawing. They provide textural and tactile interest and can indicate permanence and craftsmanship in the way they are selected and put together.

Materials with great character should be drawn as carefully and realistically as possible, but characterless materials should be left completely blank—for contrast and as a way of saving time. Corners offer excellent opportunities for showing the texture of rough materials like stone—where the material's profile can be seen.

83

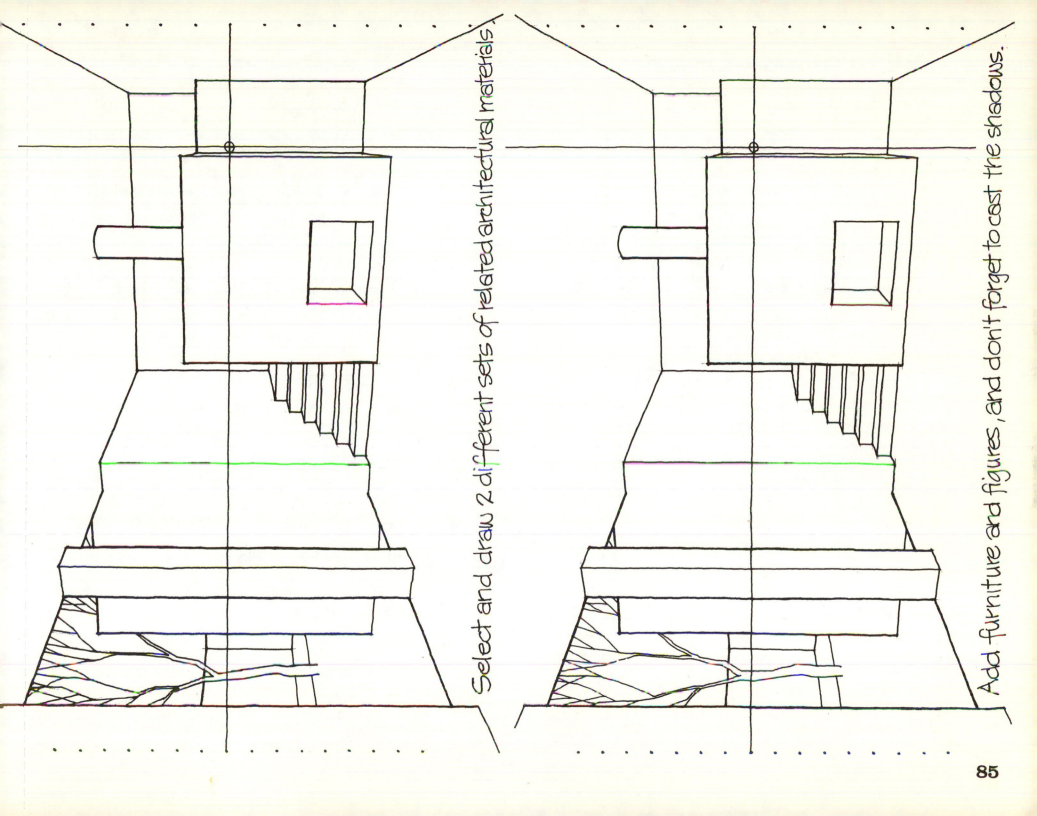

Select and draw 2 different sets of related architectural materials.

Add furniture and figures, and don't forget to cast the shadows.

REFLECTIONS

This set of exercises is designed to help students learn to draw reflections in water, glass and other reflective materials. Reflectivity is often the strongest characteristic of a material, and to render glass or water as either transparent or opaque is to misunderstand them as materials.

In drawing reflections in vertical glass surfaces there are two different realms which are reflected. One is between the viewer and the glass, and is seen both in reality and as a reflection. The second realm is that behind the viewer which is seen _only_ as reflection.

Glass Reflections

- Pull everything which is in front of the glass perpendicularly back through the glass.

- Draw these reflections as if they were the same distance (foreshortened) behind the glass as they actually are in front of the glass.

- Indicate all reflections on the glass with vertical tones of lines, since the reflecting glass surface is vertical.

- Tone reflections of objects between the viewer and the glass the same relative darkness or lightness as they are in the drawing.

- Tone reflections of everything behind the viewer as progressively lighter layers of receding space.

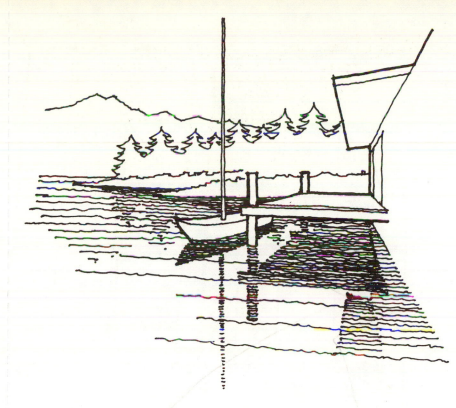

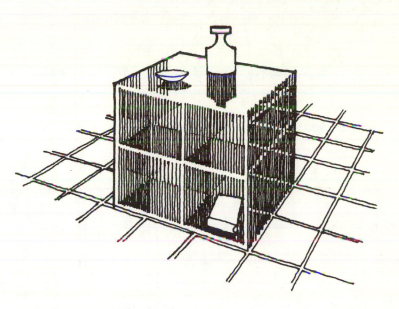

Water Reflections

- Pull everything which is above the surface of the water down through the water vertically.

- Draw these reflections as if they were the same distance below the water as they actually are above.

- Indicate all reflections on the water with crossways horizontal tones of lines since the reflecting water surface is horizontal.

- Tone reflections the same relative darkness or lightness as they are in the drawing.

Reflective Materials

- Pull everything which is in front of or above a reflective surface back or down through the surface, in a direction perpendicular to the surface.

- Draw it as if it were the same distance behind or below the reflective surface as it is in front of or above the surface.

- Indicate all reflections on the reflecting surfaces with vertical lines.

- Generally, hatch reflections of objects which are closest to the reflecting surface darkest and objects farthest from the surface lightest.

Cast the shadows from the 21 shadow angles given and render the reflections in the glass and in the water.

88

Draw the reflections in the windows.

ADDITIONAL INTEREST

Additional interest is the kind of interest that we, or nature, add to the built environment: trees, plants, furniture and the human figure itself. These elements can specify the scale, indicate the use and demonstrate the space of any environment represented in a design drawing. Their placement in a drawing should be careful not to hide space-defining intersections so that they obscure an understanding of the space; and they should never preempt the design of the environment by being self-consciously designed or drawn. The two approaches are to draw completely characterless cars, chairs, etc. or specific, well-known models so that they never compete with the design of the environment.

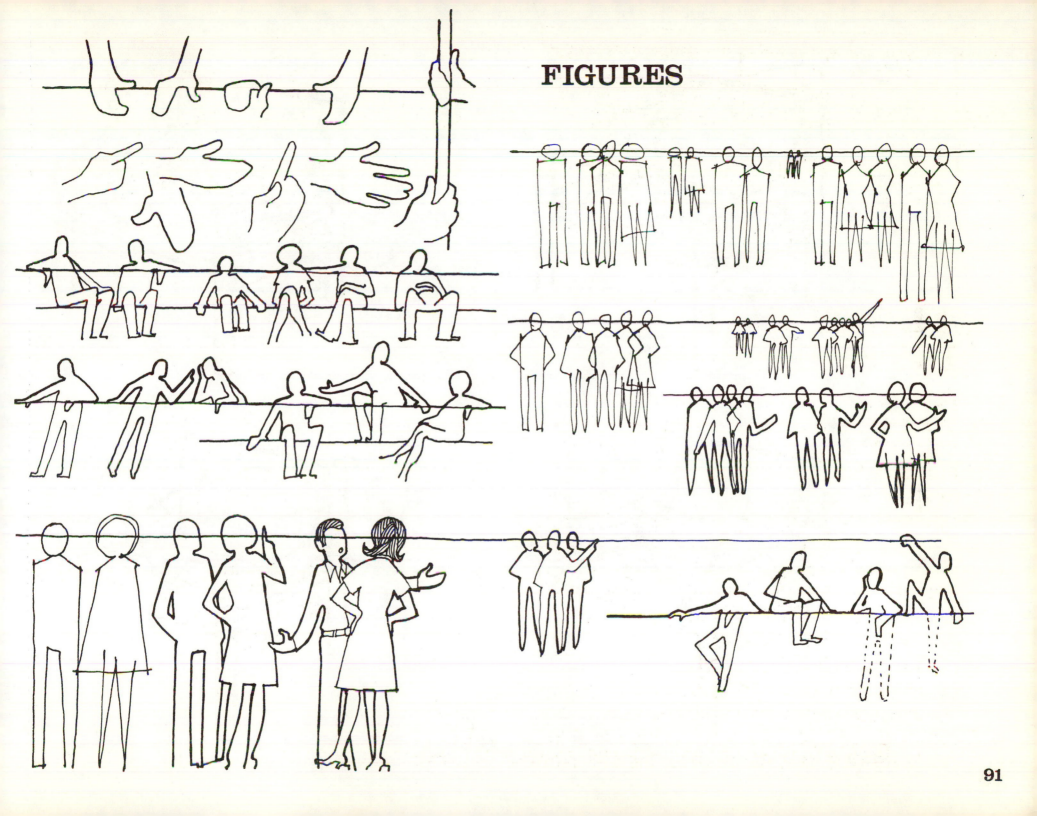

FIGURES

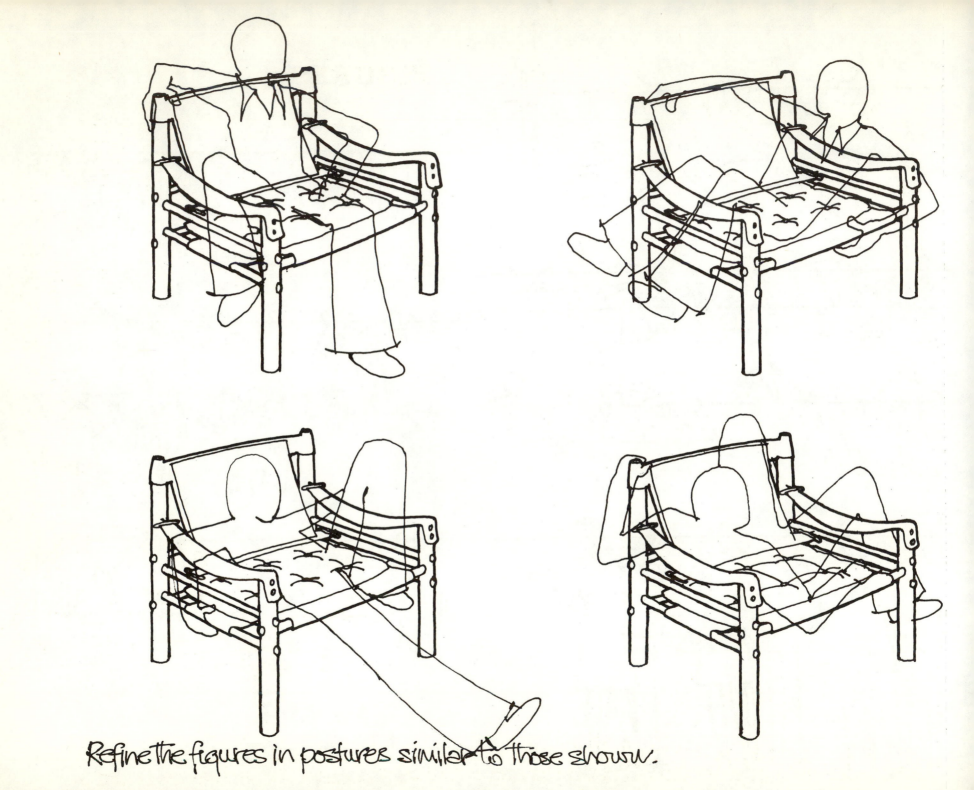

Refine the figures in postures similar to those shown.

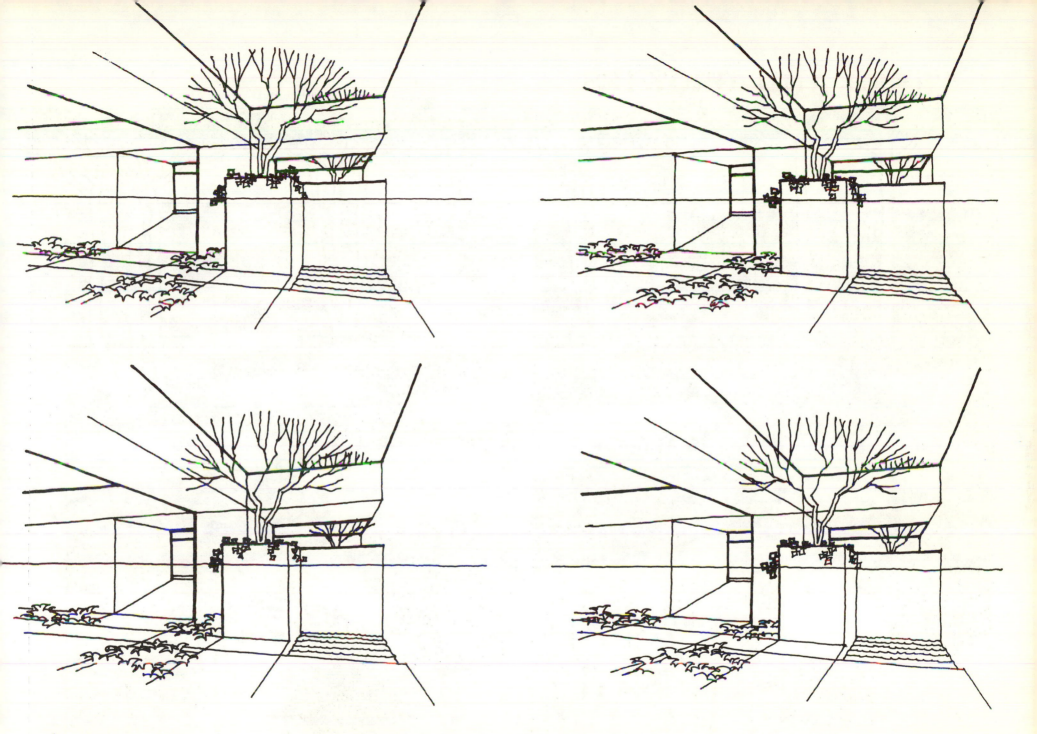

Add four different arrangements of human figures, taking care not to obscure important space-defining intersections. Change whatever will better accept the groups of figures.

93

TREES AND GROWIES

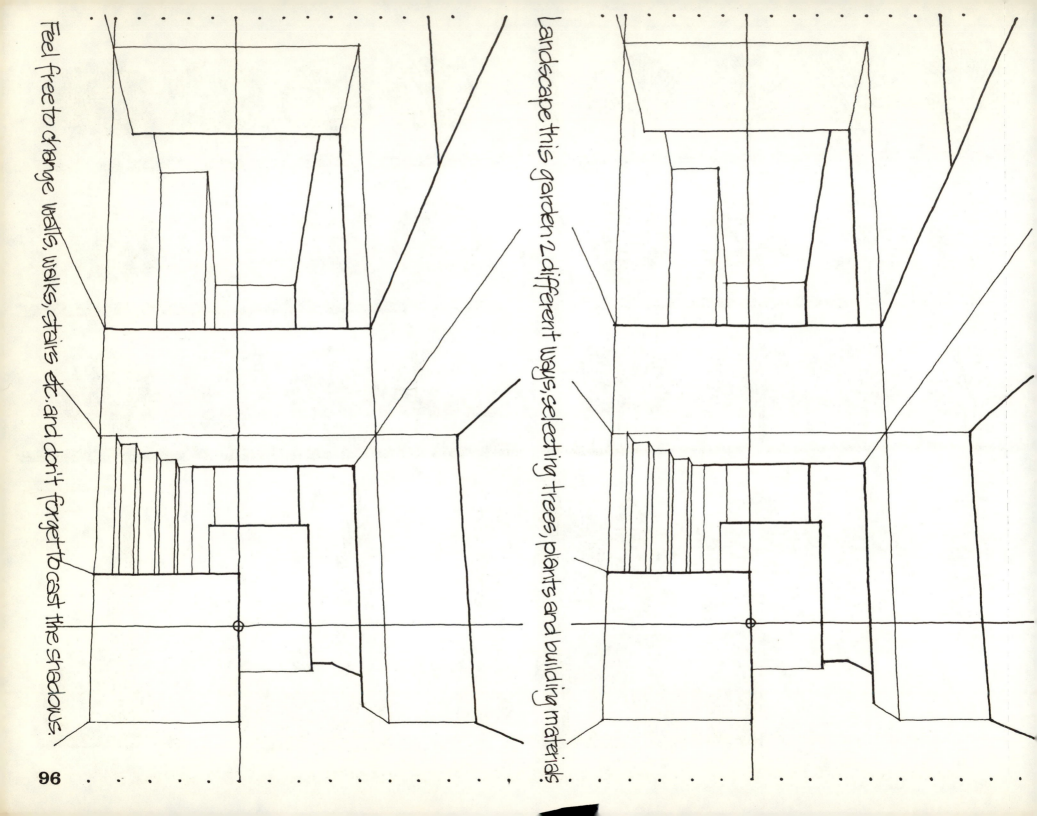

Feel free to change walls, walks, stairs etc. and don't forget to cast the shadows.

Landscape this garden 2 different ways, selecting trees, plants and building materials.

Landscape this space with a diverse collection of trees and growies. Select materials also.   **97**

FURNITURE

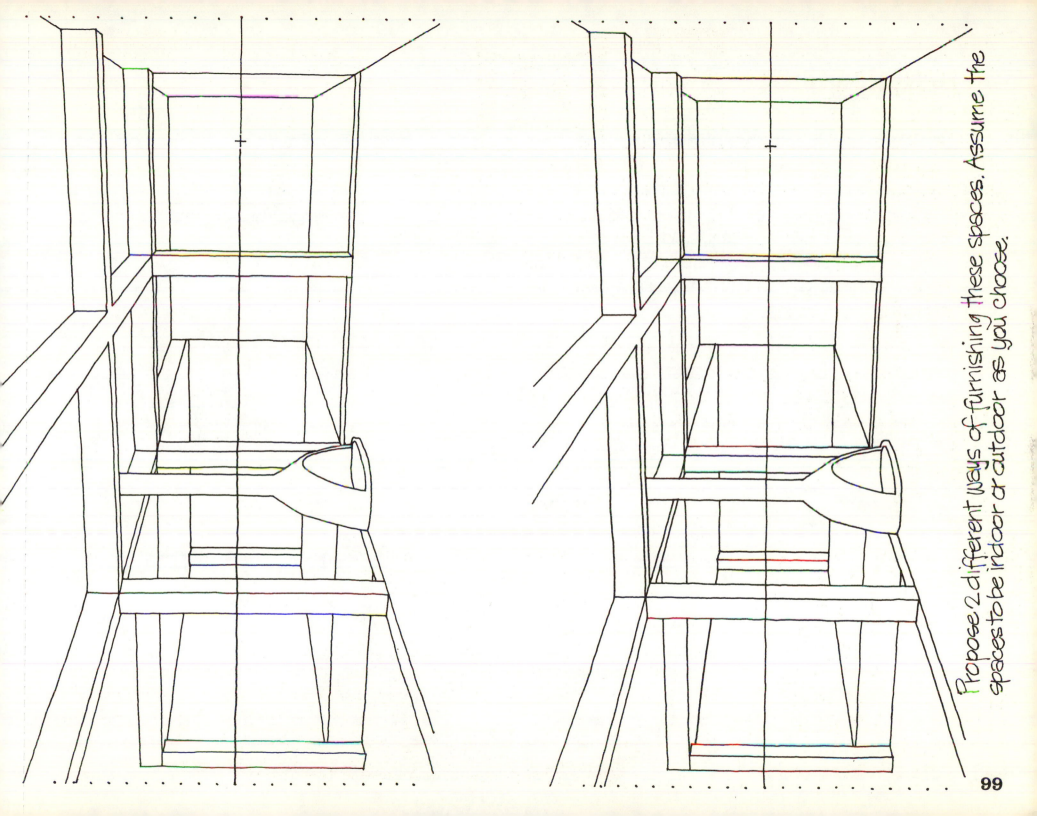

Propose 2 different ways of furnishing these spaces. Assume the spaces to be indoor or outdoor as you choose.

CONTEXT

In most representational drawings the context may be divided into foreground and background, assuming that the building, garden or interior is the middleground. The goal of both foreground and background is to extend the space of the drawing by articulating advancing and receding layers of space.

This effect is easily accomplished in the background by simply indicating layers of hedges, trees, buildings and mountains that disappear and reappear behind the patio or building, or through its windows in an interior.

The foreground has two additional problems. First, it must be made to lie down by rendering side to side horizontal textures — grass, hedges, walks, contours etc. — getting denser in the distance so that the ground plane appears to be a receding horizontal plane. The second problem is to articulate the space of the foreground without hiding the building. This is best done with vertical objects — trees, light poles, figures, etc. — that are carefully placed to avoid hiding volume-defining corners of the building.

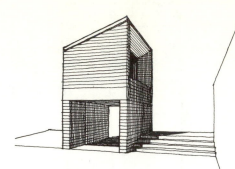

This set of exercises is designed to help students learn to indicate a realistic context for any building or environment they design. Everything we design will exist in a context and our designs will be judged partially by their relationships to their contexts. Foregrounds and backgrounds also help create the illusion of depth in a 2-dimensional drawing by indicating receding layers of space.

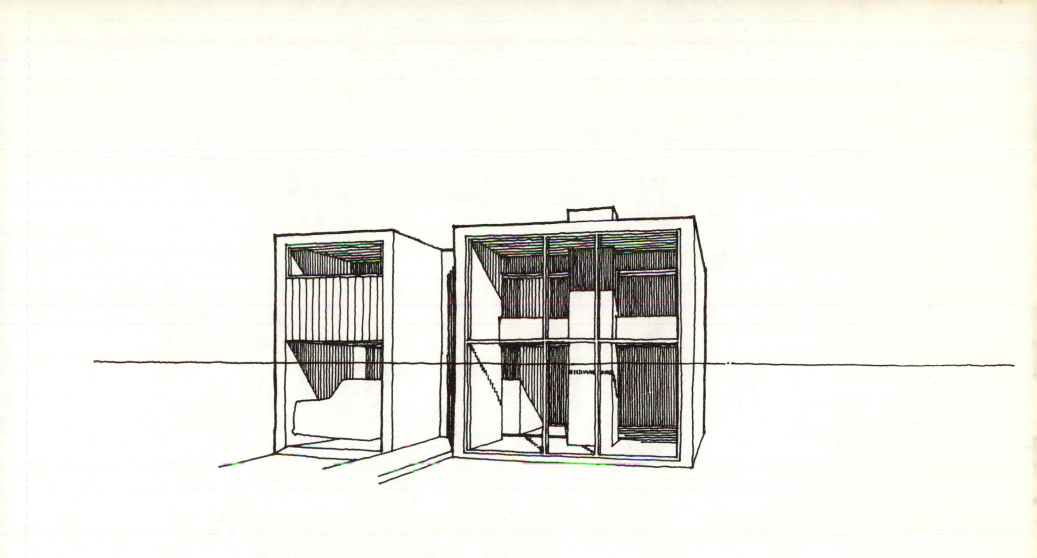

Draw a background and foreground which give this building
a believable context.

102 Draw a distant context behind the bus stop and an entirely different group of figures

WISDOM AND EFFICIENCY

Although both wisdom and speed or efficiency are largely the products of experience, there are certain techniques that can hasten the development of these attributes. The management and flexibility which the LINE AND TONE technique allows, the use of tracing paper overlays to refine a drawing, the efficiency allowed by correctly placed emphasis and the various ways in which reproduction techniques can supply technological tonal interest are worth knowing about. All these amount to a greater freedom of choice in the making of a drawing, relative to the communicative purpose of the drawing and the time available. And freedom in drawing, as in other things, comes from knowing what the options are, and having acquired the skill to make them happen.

A part of the wisdom concerning drawing includes the insight that to hold efficiency too high as a goal is antithetical to the development of drawing ability, because drawing must first become, and remain, enjoyable, or it isn't worth doing at all. The paradox is that you will only learn to draw quickly by first learning to enjoy drawing slowly.

103

LINE AND TONE'S INVESTMENT HIERARCHY

One of the unique advantages of the line and tone technique is its open-endedness. Line and tone drawings can be made in a sequence which produces an acceptable drawing quickly, but then allows you to add detail in whatever time you have left. Beyond the first stage the drawing will never look unfinished (as other techniques would) and you can return to the drawing and improve it when you have time. This investment hierarchy is best understood in terms of the drawing interest categories: spatial, tonal, textural and additional.

When a rough design sketch is selected to be made into a more finished drawing, it should first be given an accurate drafted framework, like the one at right. This underlying spatial structure is always the first investment on which everything else will stand and should include possible shadow patterns, and the placement of figures, furniture and trees, so that they will have the benefit of refinement along with everything else.

SPATIAL AND ADDITIONAL INTEREST

This spatially profiled open line drawing is the first stage of any line and tone drawing. It is very much like the simple line drawings in a child's coloring book, but everything is spatially defined, and it is a very committed, unequivocal drawing.

Spatial interest and the items of additional interest are tightly interrelated. The number of hidden spaces and spatial layers or laps should be maximized and objects of additional interest should demonstrate the space without hiding space-defining intersections (like the tree or the upper frame). The drawing communicates the environment while stopping short of the two most time-consuming interest categories.

What has been drawn is also a sound investment in the hierarchy because the time taken to make an accurate perspective framework and a studied integration with objects of additional interest will never have to be reinvested. If there is the need or opportunity to continue or return to the drawing, this solid initial investment will support the remaining interest categories which add tone and texture.

SPATIAL AND ADDITIONAL INTEREST

This spatially profiled open line drawing is the first stage of any line and tone drawing. It is very much like the simple line drawings in a child's coloring book, but everything is spatially defined, and it is a very committed, unequivocal drawing.

Spatial interest and the items of additional interest are tightly interrelated. The number of hidden spaces and spatial layers or laps should be maximized and objects of additional interest should demonstrate the space without hiding space-defining intersections (like the tree or the upper figure). The drawing communicates the environment while stopping short of the two most time-consuming interest categories.

What has been drawn is also a sound investment in the hierarchy because the time taken to make an accurate perspective framework and a studied integration with objects of additional interest will never have to be reinvested. If there is the need or opportunity to continue or return to the drawing, this solid initial investment will support the remaining interest categories which add tone and texture.

106

TONAL INTEREST

The two remaining interest categories are both very time-consuming. Tonal interest should be next because its main source – light – is not as arbitrary as the main source of textual interest–material-ials – and because tonal interest lends itself to various technological shortcuts (see REPRODUCTION TECHNIQUES page 128)

Ozalid prints, drawing on middletone paper, mounting a tracing paper drawing on a black background and then color-ing on the back with white prismacolor or mounting white paper cutouts beneath are some of the shortcuts.

In this technique the tones, including color, should be smooth, flat and characterless. Don't draw or render with the tone-mak-ing tools. All such rendering should be done with the pen. This will preserve the distinc-tion between edge-indicating lines drawn with a pen and surface indicating tones drawn with a pencil or marker.

The pattern of the tonal interest – the shade and shadows is also a matter of your choice and deserves careful study because it can do wonders to make a space read and it should be carefully interrelated with figures etc.

TONAL INTEREST

The two remaining interest categories are both very time-consuming. Tonal interest should be next because its main source -light- is not as arbitrary as the main source of textural interest-materials - and because tonal interest lends itself to various technological shortcuts (see REPRODUCTION TECHNIQUES page 128)

Ozalid prints, drawing on middletone paper, mounting a tracing paper drawing on a black background and then coloring on the back with white prismacolor or mounting white paper cutouts beneath are some of the shortcuts.

In this technique the tones, including color, should be smooth, flat and characterless. Don't draw or render with the tone-making tools. All such rendering should be done with the pen. This will preserve the distinction between edge-indicating lines drawn with a pen and surface indicating tones drawn with a pencil or marker.

The pattern of the tonal interest -the shade and shadows is also a matter of your choice and deserves careful study because it can do wonders to make a space read and it should be carefully integrated with figures etc.

TEXTURAL INTEREST

In the hierarchy suggested here, textural interest is the last category to be added. This is because the addition of textural interest is very time-consuming and, unlike tonal interest, it must be applied by hand with no technological shortcuts. It also tends to be the interest category most subject to change since its main sources - materials - are often considered late in the design decision-making process and frequently are matters for adjustment in meeting the construction budget.

In line and toned drawings, textural interest should be applied only with a pen, and applied first to the space-defining surfaces beginning with the floor or ground plane. These surfaces should always be rendered continuously because intermittent texturing will destroy the perception of the surface as the continuous background with which all spatial perception begins. Objects standing in front of these textured surfaces should never be textured but remain open silhouettes, so that the viewer's perception always continues past them to the textured surface beyond.

TEXTURAL INTEREST

In the hierarchy suggested here, textural interest is the last category to be added. This is because the addition of textural interest is very time-consuming and, unlike tonal interest, it must be applied by hand with no technological shortcuts. It also tends to be the interest category most subject to change since its main sources - materials - are often considered late in the design decision-making process and frequently are matters for adjustment in meeting the construction budget.

In line and tone drawings, textural interest should be applied only with a pen, and applied first to the space-defining surfaces beginning with the floor or ground plane. These surfaces should always be rendered continuously because intermittent texturing will destroy the perception of the surface as the continuous background with which all spatial perception begins. Objects standing in front of these textured surfaces should never be textured but remain open silhouettes, so that the viewer's perception always continues past them to the textured surface beyond.

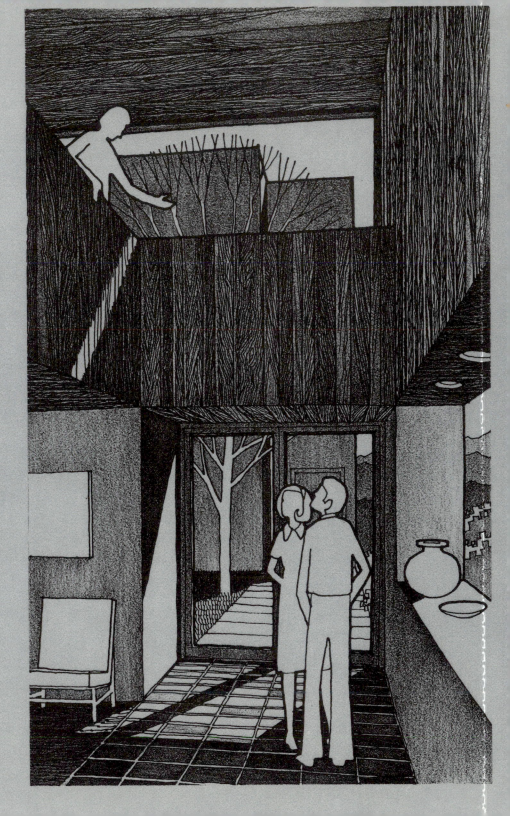

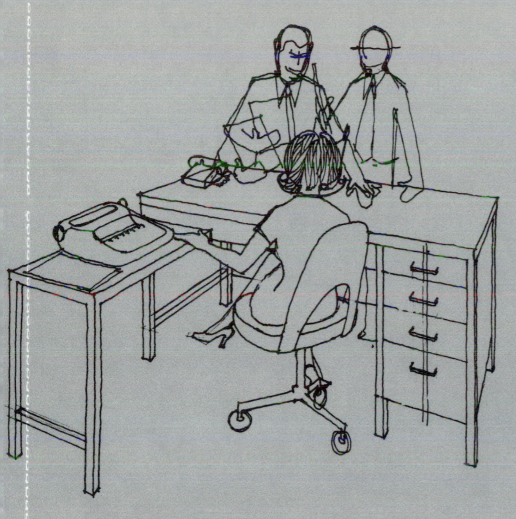

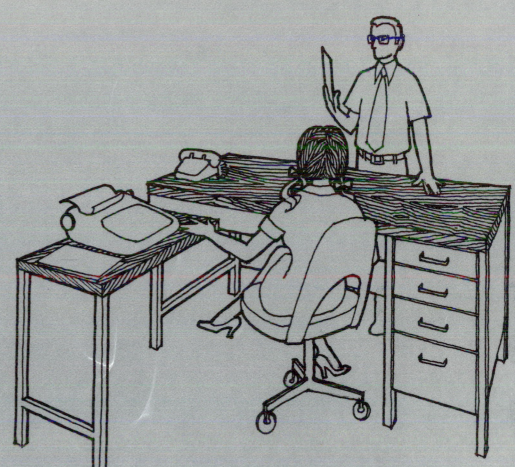

The desk and chair are now O.K. The figures need more refinement and the telephone needs to be moved so it doesn't hide the corner of the desk. The woman's ankle and hair are still awkward and the 2 men are redundant. Keys on the typewriter are redundant, and I probably won't be able to draw them well at this scale.

Not bad, but woman's hand was better in the previous sketch, and human situation seems a little male chauvinistic. Woman's hair texture too much. ...conflicts with wood grain.... but that's all the time I have now.

The desk and chair are now O.K. The figures need more refinement and the telephone needs to be moved so it doesn't hide the corner of the desk. The woman's ankle and hair are still awkward and the 2 men are redundant. Keys on the type- writer are redundant, and I probab- ly won't be able to draw them well at this scale.

Not bad, but woman's hand was better in the previous sketch, and human situation seems a little male chauvin- istic. Woman's hair texture too much ...conflicts with wood grain.... but that's all the time I have now.

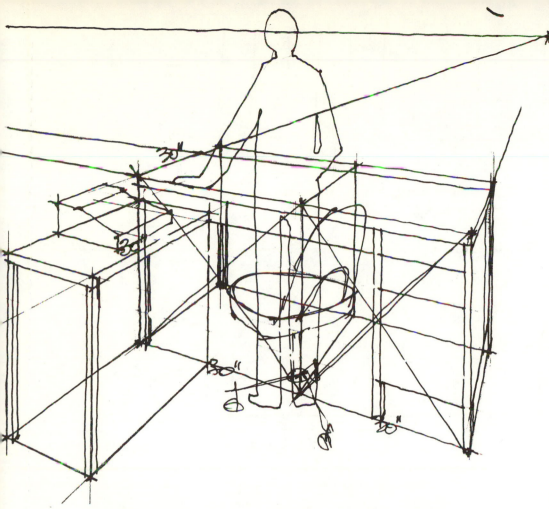

OVERLAID REFINEMENT

This set of experiences is designed to help students develop the ability to refine a crude sketch into a series of more resolved drawings by overlaying the first rough sketches with successive layers of tracing paper.

Designers should learn to visualize any design drawing, not as a single drawing, but as a potential stack of drawings progressing from a very crude sketch at the bottom to a very slick, detailed rendering at the top layer. When you have the disciplined ability to raise any rough sketch to these various levels, drawing becomes a matter of free choice, depending on the purpose of the drawing and the time available.

It takes awhile to develop the skill and confidence to refine a rough sketch and know where you're going with it... and it's always tempting to try to make a drawing halfway up the stack without the supporting underlays. The drawing and placement of figures, trees and shadows always need the benefit of overlaid refinement.

Refinement of any design drawing depends on working over an accurate spatial structure or perspective framework. This is absolutely basic. No amount of beautiful drawing over a distorted or inaccurate framework will produce an acceptable result because the distortions and inaccuracies will still be there.

You are much wiser to invest the time to make an accurate perspective framework.

113

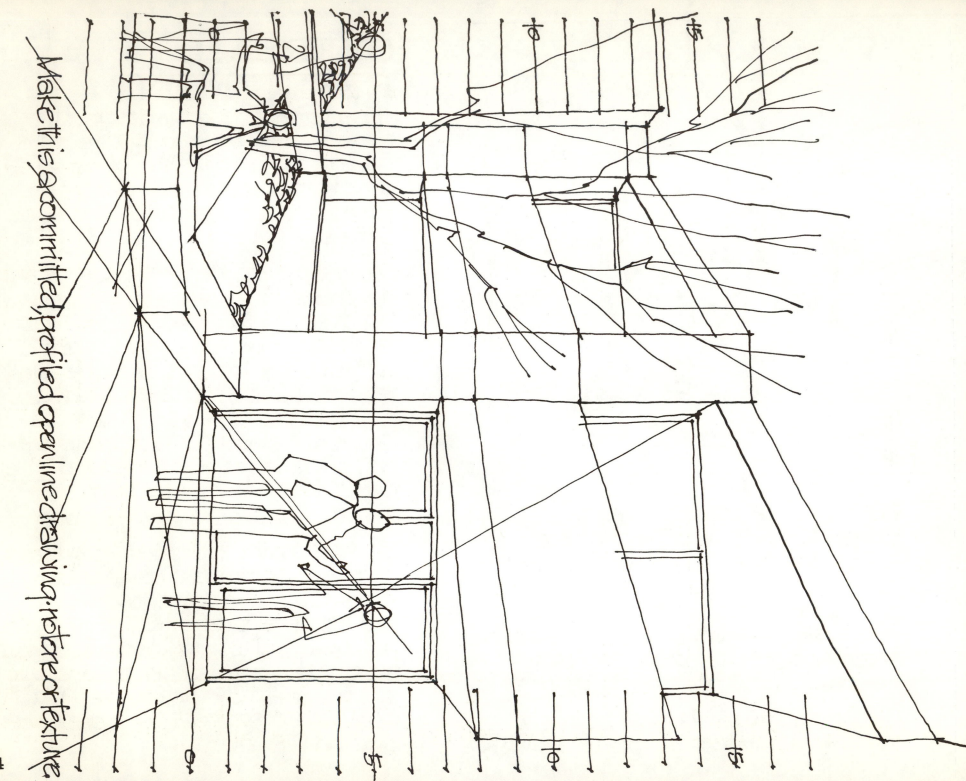

Make this a committed, profiled open line drawing. not a tone or texture.

114

Make a committed, profiled open line drawing limited to spatial & figural interest.

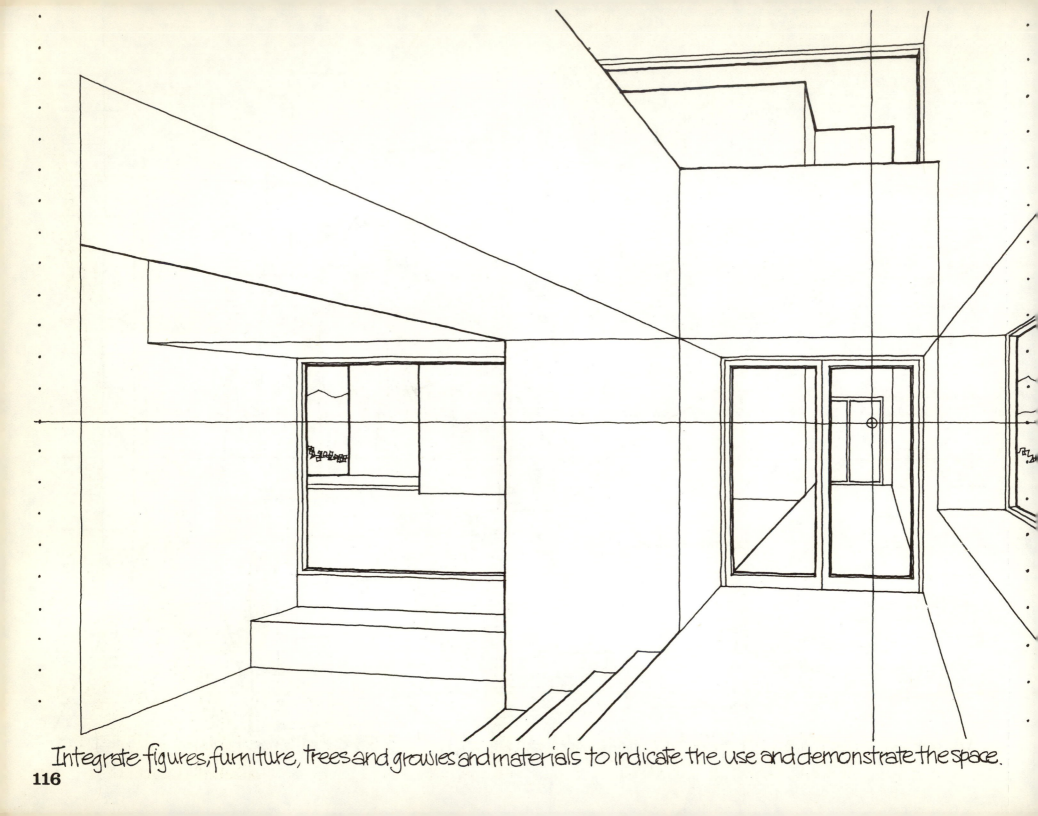

Integrate figures, furniture, trees and growies and materials to indicate the use and demonstrate the space.

Add textural interest

117

What would the most dramatic sun angle be?

wall? materials

should railing be open or solid

solid? or cut away to show form of the stair?

fountain? or waterfall from upper level?

? pool or planter

? paving material

Refine this design for a split-level courtyard. Hand in interim overlays with the final drawing.

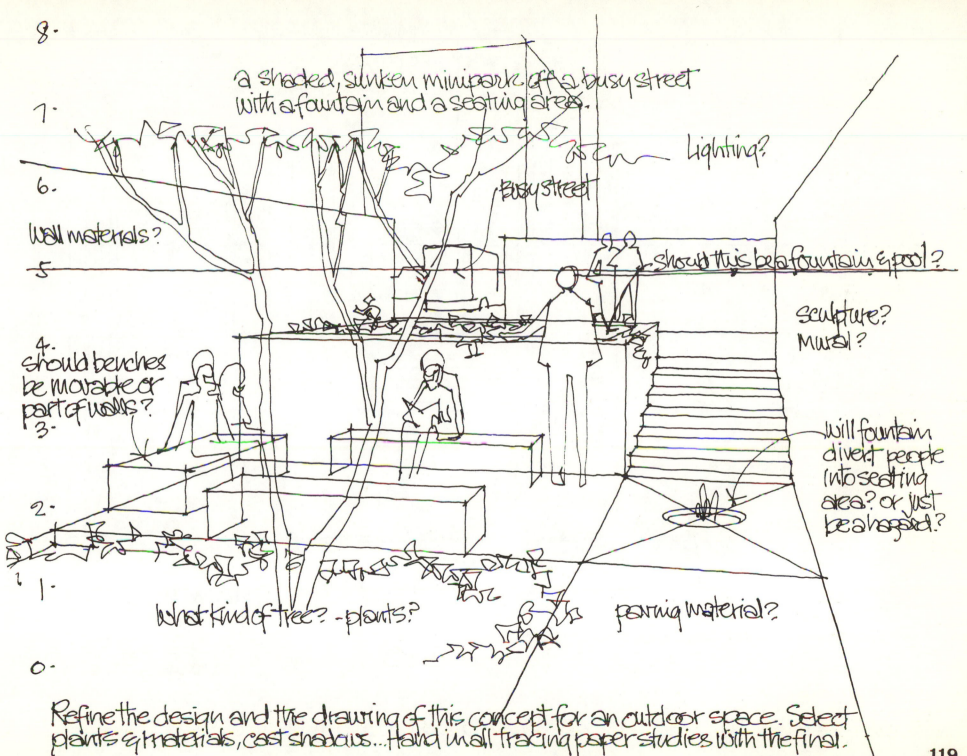

8.

a shaded, sunken minipark off a busy street
with a fountain and a seating area.

7.

Lighting?

6.

busy street

Wall materials?

5.

should this be a fountain & pool?

sculpture?
Mural?

4.
should benches
be movable or
part of walls?

3.

Will fountain
divert people
into seating
area? or just
be a hazard?

2.

1.

What kind of tree? - plants?

paving material?

0.

Refine the design and the drawing of this concept for an outdoor space. Select
plants & materials, cast shadows... Hand in all tracing paper studies with the final.

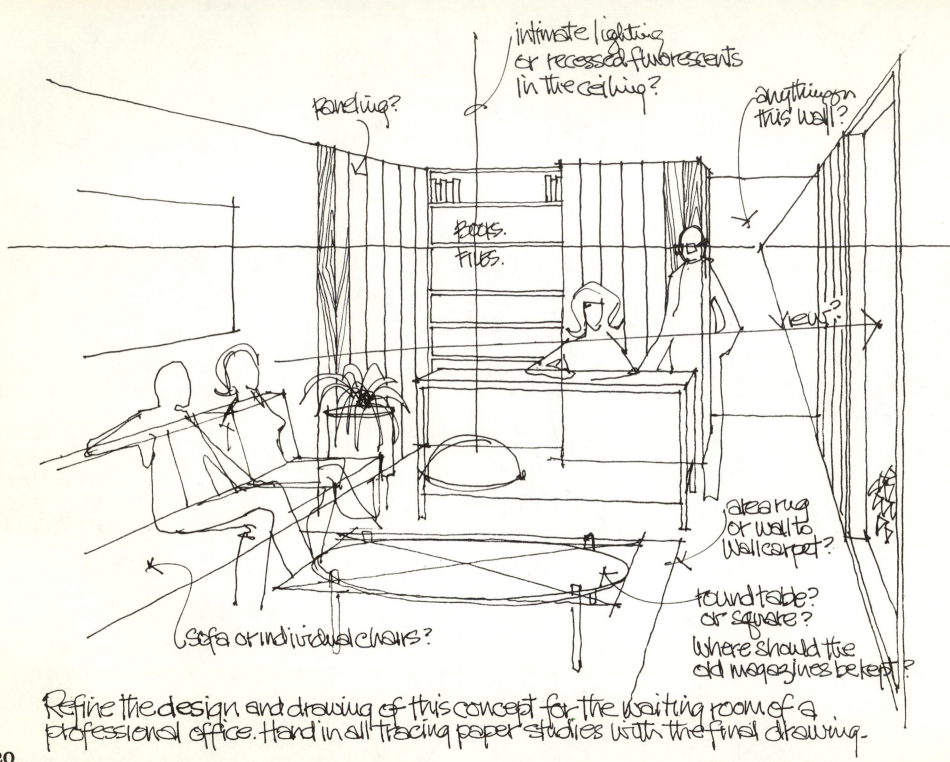

intimate lighting
or recessed fluorescents
in the ceiling?

paneling?

anything on
this wall?

BOOKS.
FILES.

view?

area rug
or wall to
wall carpet?

round table?
or square?

Where should the
old magazines be kept?

sofa or individual chairs?

Refine the design and drawing of this concept for the waiting room of a
professional office. Hand in all tracing paper studies with the final drawing.

EMPHASIS

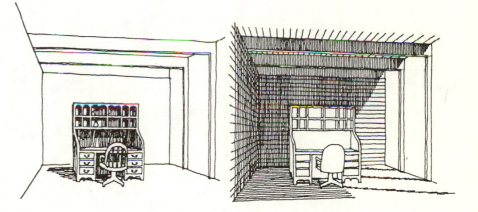

This set of experiences is designed to help students understand the variety of empha- ses which a drawing may have by shifting the emphasis of a given drawing in an as- signed direction or in the direction of a particular design discipline: Architecture, Landscape Architecture or Interior Design.

Correctly placed emphasis can focus the designers' attention on the area for which they are responsible and avoid the dissi- pation of design effort into areas beyond their concern.

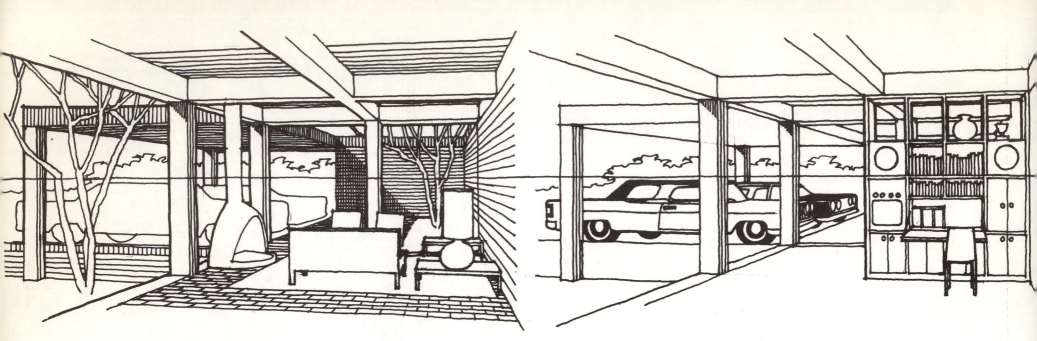

ARCHITECTURAL DESIGN

This drawing is intended to show what might be the correct emphasis for an architectural design drawing. Drawing effort, especially textural interest is concentrated on the space-defining surfaces, emphasizing the structural elements and the architectural materials. The rendering effort is on the spatial container with the furniture and trees left as unrendered outlines, and placed carefully so that they never hide the volume-defining intersections of wall, ceiling and floor.

INDUSTRIAL DESIGN

This drawing is intended to show what might be the correct emphasis for an industrial design drawing. Drawing effort is concentrated on the industrial products - the automobiles and the storage wall - and they are given prominence by their placement in the drawing. The architectural surfaces, the exterior landscaping and other furnishings are either eliminated or drawn in the simplest possible way.

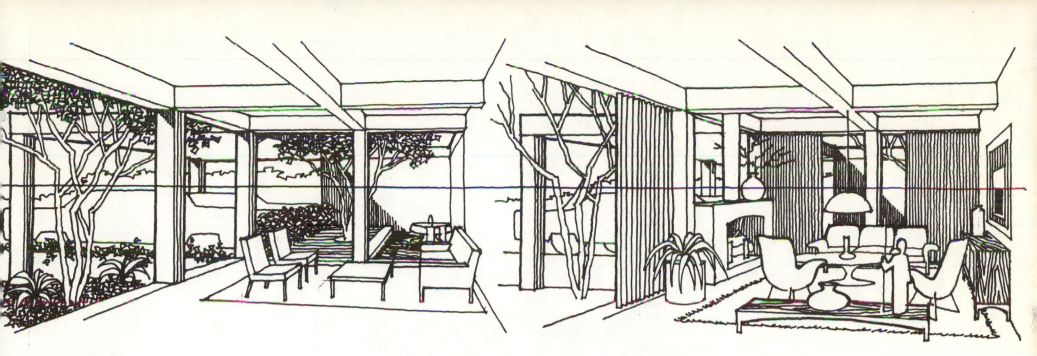

LANDSCAPE DESIGN

This drawing is intended to show what might be the correct emphasis for a landscape design drawing. Drawing effort, especially textural and figural interest is concentrated on the exterior spaces, trees and plants. The furniture has little design character and is kept to a bare minimum and the architectural surfaces and the furniture are left as unrendered outlines.

INTERIOR DESIGN

This drawing is intended to show what might be the correct emphasis for an interior design drawing. Drawing effort, especially textural and figural interest, is concentrated on the interior space. The furniture, drapes, carpeting and accessories are selected and drawn with more design character, while the architectural surfaces and the exterior spaces are left as unrendered outlines. The interior furnishings are also given prominence in their placement, not hesitating to cover up architectural details or exterior spaces.

123

Change the emphasis of this drawing from the architecture to the landscaping.

Change the drawing to give it emphasis in an assigned direction: landscaping, architecture, furniture etc.

Change the drawing to give it emphasis in an assigned direction – the ceiling, the floor and splash tile, the cabinets etc.

Add any assigned set of drawing interest categories: spatial, tonal, textural or figural.

REPRODUCTION TECHNIQUES

This set of experiences is designed to help students learn the options offered by today's technology in the reproduction of drawings. Some reproduction techniques are great time-savers, while others can help you produce very slick, professional-looking renderings, and all offer the great advantage of preserving the original drawing for future modification or further reproduction.

The greatest saving in time which reproduction techniques afford is the various ways they can be used to produce middletone drawings-the most dramatic being night perspectives. The simplest form of this is to make a mylar print or a Xerox print on tracing paper and mount the print on a dark board. This will immediately have the effect of making the drawing into a middletone drawing, and white prismacolor or white paper cutouts can then be added to the underside of the transparent print. This technique also works well for plans and sections. Another way to obtain a good middletone drawing from an ink line tracing is to simply have a quality Xerox copy run on a middletone paper of your choice. .....a product which until recently could only be produced very laboriously or expensively.

Perhaps the most popular reproduction technique used in making presentation drawings is still OZALID process prints on various papers...sepia, brown line, black line or mylar at various speeds, with prismacolor or felt tip markers applied to the resulting print. Underexposure of the various papers, especially sepia and brown line will produce a beautiful brown tone, effortlessly, even where the paper was white. Usually this bonus print tone is assumed to be the value of shade, with shadows rendered darker before the print is made. The subsequent addition of the light tones - sunlit surfaces, sky and sky reflections make a very dramatic rendering. Instructions are given on the following drawings so that students may have a brief exposure to what various reproduction techniques can do.

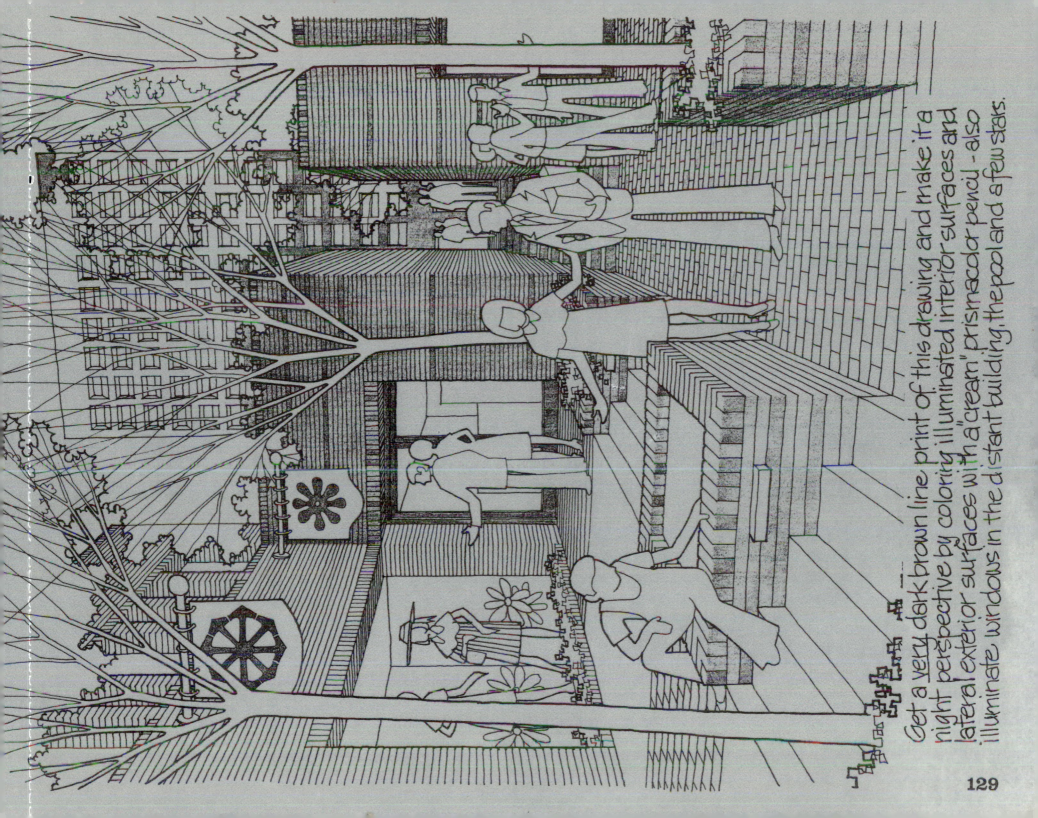

Get a _very_ dark brown line print of this drawing and make it a night perspective by coloring illuminated interior surfaces and lateral exterior surfaces with a "cream" prismacolor pencil - also illuminate windows in the distant building, the pool and a few stars.

Continuing with the same drawing toward a daytime perspective, you would cast shadows and add glass reflections like this; get a medium brown line print and then color the sky, sky reflections, and sunlit surfaces.

131

Get a medium brown line print and try a 2-coat coloring of the brick - prisma color orange under madder red varying different bricks and courses.

133

Get a nice line brown like that and a thin 2-coat coloring of the blackbird. Use a dark orange under where the two different things meet, and a color orange under where the two shades and corners.

Get a mylar print (matte back or wrong reading on the emulsion) and apply prismacolor to the back.

135

get a mylar print (matte back or wrong reading on the emulsion) and apply prismacolor to the back.

135

BLACK AND WHITE ON MIDDLETONE

The middletone pages which follow are duplicates of selected previous experiences. They are included to allow students to try making black and white on middletone drawings. Until recently this technique demanded the rather tedious step of transferring a tracing paper drawing to opaque middletone paper. Now, however, there are duplicating machines which will produce a high quality copy (of limited size) from a tracing paper sketch on a middletone paper of your choice.

Note: The intermittent page numbers which follow do not mean the book is incomplete or defective. Only selected exercises are repeated here and their earlier page numbers are repeated for easy reference.

Continuing with the same drawing toward a daytime perspective, you would cast shadows and add glass reflections like this; get a medium brown line print and then color the sky, sky reflections, and sunlit surfaces.

Get a medium brown line print and try a 2-coat coloring of the brick - prisma color orange under madder red varying different bricks and courses.

141

Get a mylar print (matte back or wrong reading on the emulsion) and apply prismacolor to the back.

143